Global Solutions for Multilingual Applications

Global Solutions for Multilingual Applications
Real-World Techniques for Developers and Designers

Chris Ott

Wiley Computer Publishing

John Wiley & Sons, Inc.

NEW YORK • CHICHESTER • WEINHEIM • BRISBANE • SINGAPORE • TORONTO

Editor: Cary Sullivan

Managing Editor: Marnie Wielage

Electronic Products, Associate Editor: Mike Sosa

Text Design & Composition: North Market Street Graphics

Library of Congress Cataloging-in-Publication Data:
Ott, Christopher, 1970–
    Global solutions for multilingual applications : real world
  techniques for developers and designers / Christopher Ott.
        p.   cm.
      ISBN 0-471-34827-9 (paper/website : alk. paper)
      1. Multilingual computing.   2. Application software—Development.
    I. Title.
    QA76.9.M68088   1999
    004—dc21   99-35174
                                                                    CIP

Printed in the United States of America.

10 9 8 7 6 5 4 3 2 1

For my grandmother, Florence Lashua.

CONTENTS

Maybe we should blame it on English.

Some of the most important early work with personal computer technology was done in English and for use in English, which is a somewhat peculiar language. English uses a relatively small number of characters, it is unidirectional (left to right), and it is even one of the few languages that can be written without diacritics, such as accent marks. All of these things make it comparatively easier for computers to handle English than most other languages, some of which require support for larger numbers of characters, diacritics that modify characters, and support for bidirectional (left-to-right and right-to-left) input.

In other words, computers have generally been designed to work with one of the world's simplest languages (at least from a computing standpoint) and not the more complex ones. The result is that using computers with other languages can be particularly complicated.

Depending on the kind of work you do—as a Webmaster, a developer, an IT manager, a tech-support representative, an educator or student trying to teach or learn another language, a translator, or anyone else who simply needs to be able to use computers in languages other than English—language adds a new dimension to your work. At times it can be difficult to find answers to even basic questions about multilingual computing, and cutting-edge fields are made even more complicated by the need to support multiple languages.

At the same time, these questions are becoming more important. Operating systems, applications, and the Internet were generally designed to work first and best with English, but this is changing quickly. To succeed in the increasingly global market, applications must support all the languages of the world, and the World Wide Web must do a better job of living up to the global reach of its name. By far, the most commonly used language on the Internet today is still English (trailed by a few other Western European languages and Japanese), but this will change as technology becomes more and more widely used around the world in regions that do not even primarily use the Latin alphabet, much less English. Languages that will undoubtedly make up a greater part of the world's electronic communication than they do today include Chinese, Japanese, Korean, Arabic, Russian, and Hindi. And while English is well established as a kind of international language, there is no reason to believe that other major languages are going to fade away or that there is no need for software to support them.

If language touches on the work that you do, this book is designed to offer solutions for the multilingual computing issues that arise. It is meant to give an overview of the subject and offer techniques for those who develop multilingual applications and Web sites, but it is also meant to provide answers for those who make decisions about, support, and use multilingual applications.

How This Book Is Organized

This book is divided into three parts. Part One, "Multilingual Basics," describes what is needed for basic multilingual support and compatibility. Part Two, "Developing Multilingual Applications and International Solutions," discusses strategies and techniques for creating applications and other resources, as well as providing more truly multilingual computing support within global organizations. Part Three, "Multilingual Communications and Content," offers additional advice on multilingual support for what is driving so much of our technological growth: the need to communicate and create content for the entire world, not just speakers of English.

Chapter 1, "The World-Ready Computer," provides advice for setting up computers—mainly PCs and Macintoshes—for use with fonts, language kits, and other resources. Advice is broken down by major language groups, with platform-specific advice about where to obtain the software that is needed for language support.

Chapter 2, "World-Savvy Applications," gives an overview of the multilingual capabilities of productivity applications, such as word processors, as well as Web browsers, databases, and optical character recognition (OCR) software.

Chapter 3, "Multilingual Compatibility Issues," describes the new text standard, Unicode, which promises to make the exchange of multilingual information easier. It also provides advice on how to share multilingual documents more easily across different platforms.

Chapter 4, "Language to Go: Keeping Connected While Traveling," is meant especially for travelers who need to stay connected to the Internet no matter where in the world they are, and who also need to act as their own multilingual tech-support staff when support from their home offices isn't available.

Chapter 5, "Strategies for Multilingual Development and Internationalization," discusses the major issues involved in developing multilingual products for the global market, as well as how to make choices and plans that will carry you and your organization into a more multilingual future.

Chapter 6, "Developing Multilingual Applications," discusses the major issues that need to be kept in mind when developing multilingual applications, along with details about the multilingual capabilities of major platforms and an overview of tools that are available to make multilingual development easier.

Chapter 7, "Creating and Converting Multilingual Resources," offers advice and techniques for creating resources, such as fonts and keyboards, which may not already exist for languages that you need to support. It also provides details on how to convert existing data from one language encoding to another.

Chapter 8, "Translation and Localization," examines the issues involved in preparing applications and other materials (such as documentation) for different locales worldwide. There is also an overview of tools for translators, tools for localization, and options for automatic translation.

Chapter 9, "Multilingual Electronic Communication," discusses the options for making multilingual electronic communication easier, with a focus on email, as well as newsreaders, the use of interactive Web forms with non-Latin text, and multilingual personal digital assistants.

Chapter 10, "Multilingual Publishing, Graphic Design, and Multimedia," looks at the multilingual aspects of work in these fields, with a look at the major issues involved in each, and the applications and tools that can help you put multilingual work in print or on screen.

Chapter 11, "Creating Multilingual Internet and Intranet Sites," discusses the major issues to keep in mind when developing multilingual intranet sites for global organizations, and multilingual Internet sites for a global audience. It also provides information about some of the best tools available to do this.

Who Should Read This Book?

This book has been written primarily with intermediate-level Webmasters, developers, and IT managers in mind—people who already have a technical background but who may not be familiar with language issues and how they affect their work. Specific information about multilingual development strategies is provided in Part Two, and techniques for specific fields such as Web publishing are provided in Part Three. Readers who are already familiar with the basics of multilingual support may want to skip directly to these parts.

For those who need a more complete background, as well as how-to help, Part One offers an entry-level look at the subject that provides the information needed to get working in any language.

It is worth noting that although this book provides plenty of details for Windows users, it gives roughly equal coverage to the Macintosh. This is because the Mac, even though it has a much smaller market share than Windows, has a number of unique and important features which suit it well for multilingual use, and which are not yet readily available in Windows. This will begin to change with the debut of Microsoft Windows 2000, but for now, multilingual use is a strong niche market for Apple, in which the Mac has noteworthy advantages. More limited details are provided for users of other operating systems, such as Linux, BeOS, and OS/2, as well.

Tools You Will Need

No particular tools are needed to use this book, but Internet access will be very helpful. The book's companion Web site at www.wiley.com/compbooks/ott provides links to the sites for all products and resources discussed or mentioned in the book. Many forms of multilingual support—fonts, keyboard layouts, different languages, versions of applications such as Web browsers, and so forth—can be freely downloaded, and there are links to sites that showcase multilingual techniques, as well. The book's companion site will also include additions and corrections that were not possible to include in the book itself.

What This Book Aims to Do

My own familiarity with the field of multilingual computing comes from three years as the technical coordinator of the Center for Language Studies at Brown University, from 1993 to 1996. Faculty, staff, and students were involved in a range of work that included the use of everyday applications, working with data in non-Latin alphabets, creating Web pages, and developing language-education software.

One of the things that becomes immediately obvious in multilingual work is that there are few concise sources of information to turn to. While there is a wealth of information available on the Web about multilingual computing issues, as well as in articles in various publications, much of this information is scattered through dozens of sources online and in print, and much of it is tailored to individual languages or products. Not only is it sometimes difficult to get a concise overview of the major issues that affect multilingual computing, it can even be difficult to get answers to basic questions. Quite often, even the tech-support representatives of software companies that make products with multilingual capabilities are unfamiliar with the details of how multilingual support works.

This book aims to provide that concise overview and to supplement it with real-world details, techniques, and suggestions. Multilingual computing is a vast subject—it affects all computing fields, multiplied by the number of languages of the world—but this book is intended as the first source to turn to for insight, advice, and referrals to other sources of information.

ACKNOWLEDGMENTS

Thanks for help with this book are due especially to Andrea Vine, for her enthusiasm in providing answers and advice; Laurel Mittenthal, for her suggestions and comments on several chapters; Dr. Julius Krava and David Danaher for their many helpful suggestions on fonts.

Thanks are also due to Heather Alexander, Adil Allawi, F. Avery Bishop, Christina Berry, Elaine Betts, David Brooks, Lori Brownell, Brian R. Burton, Michael Cárdenas, Karen Chakmakian, Alan Cienki, Lee Collins, Tom Edwards, Bert Esselink, Ken Frank, Stephen H. Franke, Kim Freeman, Mark Foster, Bradley Gano, Jessica Garcia, Rob Garcia, Sabine Gross, Debs Hahn, Bill Hall, George N. Hallak, Chris Hanaoka, Eric Harlow, Farid Harmoush, Ted Harrison, David Herren, Andres Heuberger, Tin Kam Ho, Otmar Hoefer, Jonathan Hoefler, John Hudson, William Hultman, the International Macintosh Users Group, David Kanig, Michael Kung, Nadine Kano, Rajesh Kumar, Mark Larson, David Lemon, Kathleen Levesque, Peter Lowe, Kevin Mallon, Rebecca Manring, Kamal Mansour, Tom McCarthy, Doug McKenna, Dirk Meyer, John Meyer, Keith Mills, Wes Nakamura, Nazih Noujaim, Larry Oppenberg, Dennis Ott, Marek Pawlowski, Yucong Phease, Janet Pike, Vianna Quock, Stephanie Rasmussen, Chris Richards, Melanie Rushworth, Ben Sargent, Paula Shannon, Staci Sheppard, Seth Thomas Schneider, Tim Strait, Cary Sullivan, Debra Webster, Michel Wildoer, Misha Wolf, Sue Ellen Wright, Dovie Wylie, Emil Yakupov, Jennifer Yanez-Pastor, Rosemary Yule, Mark Zeren, James Zheng, and many others.

Naturally, responsibility for any errors, omissions, or oversights belongs to me.

I'd also like to thank the participants of the Language Learning Technology International discussion list (http://schiller.dartmouth.edu/llti), from whom I've learned a great deal over the years, as well as everyone with whom I worked at the Brown University Center for Language Studies.

Global Solutions for Multilingual Applications

PART ONE

Multilingual Basics

CHAPTER 1

The World-Ready Computer

Before you can do (or even view) any work with your computer in languages other than English, you may need to get a few things set up. This can be easy or fairly complex, all depending on what languages you want to work with.

For languages that are relatively close to English, like Spanish, German, and other Western European languages, you may need to do almost nothing, because support is generally already built in. But for extra convenience in working with these languages—and for more complex capabilities, such as work in languages that use another writing system (Chinese, for example)—you may need to buy and install additional software.

This chapter covers the basic multilingual features of Windows 98 and Mac OS 8.5. It also explains how to add support for each of the world's major languages that are not already supported in the standard U.S. English versions of the major operating systems.

NOTE
Additional details about other systems, such as Windows NT, OS/2, and Linux, as well as forthcoming systems such as Windows 2000 and Mac OS X, are provided in Chapter 3, "Multilingual Compatibility Issues."

The Basics: Built-In ASCII Support

Thanks to the American Standard Code for Information Interchange (ASCII), even a computer set up for use in English has some built-in support for working in other languages. The standard ASCII set has 128 different characters, and the extended ASCII set (introduced by IBM in 1981 and still widely used today) has an additional 128 characters, for a total of 256.

What this means is that with many English fonts, you can type as many as 256 different characters. These characters include the 26 uppercase and 26 lowercase letters of the English alphabet, the numbers 0 to 9, punctuation marks, and mathematical symbols such as the equals sign (=). They may also have characters for all Western European languages, including characters such as é, ñ, and ü.

The way that computers handle these characters in extended ASCII is different from the way that you might think of them yourself. In other words, the computer doesn't see a character like á as "a with an accent" (although this may be how it is composed for print, for example). The computer considers á to be a completely different character from a, and each character like this has its own place in the ASCII table.

NOTE

A new standard called *Unicode* is emerging as a truly global successor to ASCII and other local character sets. Unicode is discussed in detail in Chapter 3, but references to Unicode support are made in this chapter and in Chapter 2, "World-Savvy Applications."

When someone wants to know how to type one of these characters, they generally ask about "accent marks." A better term is *diacritics*, since these marks include more than just the acute accent (´) and the grave accent (`). They also include marks such as the circumflex (^) and the tilde (~). The term *diacritics* is generally used in this book to refer to these markings.

Foreign Character Basics: Windows

To see all the characters that are available in a particular font in Windows, use *Character Map* (click Start, then go to Programs, then Accessories, then System Tools). Character Map can display all the characters available for each of the fonts you have installed. Since some fonts have a different selection of characters, you can look at the character set for a different font by using the font pulldown menu within Character Map.

Characters or Glyphs?

In multilingual work, you may come across references to both *characters* and *glyphs*. The difference is that *character* refers to an entity in the abstract, like the letter *c* while *glyph* refers to the particular shape in which a character is displayed. The character *c,* for example, can be displayed in italics, with or without serifs, in a font that makes it look like it has been written in crayon, and so forth. Each of these different glyphs is a different rendering of the character *c*. This difference between characters and glyphs is especially important in languages such as Arabic, where the appearance of a character may vary depending on its position in a word.

Character Map allows you to select and copy one or more characters into the Windows clipboard to be pasted into a document you are working on in another application. Character Map also reveals the keystroke combinations needed to type any of the font's characters. For characters not included on a standard keyboard, you hold down the Alt key while typing the character's numeric code. As Figure 1.1 shows, the numeric code for the character *á* is 0225.

Using Character Map or numeric codes to enter characters from the extended ASCII set works fine if you only need to enter a few characters, but it can be cumbersome if you need to work extensively in the

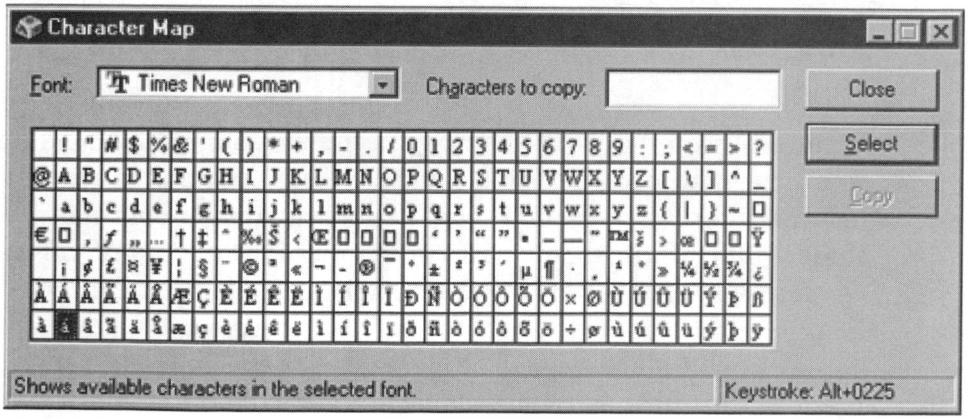

Figure 1.1   Character Map shows all the characters available in the selected font.

languages these characters are used in. Fortunately, there are more convenient ways to do this.

Some individual applications, such as Microsoft Word and Corel WordPerfect, offer their own methods for entering characters for other languages. See the documentation for the applications you use for further details.

Another solution is to choose a keyboard layout that puts foreign characters in convenient locations—usually the places they would be on the keyboards used in the country or countries where the language you are typing is spoken. See the next section for more details about keyboard layouts.

Third-party accessories are also available. One shareware option is *3-D Keyboard*, from Fingertip Software (www.fingertipsoft.com), which shows a map of your current keyboard layout and also lets you design your own layouts. For example, you could designate that the Alt key in combination with the *o* key will produce an *ö*, *ó*, *ø*, or any other character you prefer. See Chapter 7, "Creating and Converting Multilingual Resources," for more information. Other products that allow you to create macros also allow you to choose certain keys or key combinations that will type special characters for you.

The Multilanguage Capabilities of Windows

If you are searching for additional information online or in Windows Help about multilingual capabilities, it is important to know that Microsoft usually refers to multilingual features as *multilanguage* capabilities, or occasionally as *international language support*. Use these words and phrases as search keywords in addition to *multilingual* or the name of the language you are interested in.

Because the methods for entering special language characters can vary so much—and because using some key combinations to type characters can interfere with the keyboard equivalents for commands in some applications—some users prefer memorizing the ASCII codes (such as Alt+0225 for *á*), or keeping a list of the numerical codes handy. Cumbersome though this may be, these work regardless of the application you are using. The codes for special characters required by Western European languages is included in Table 1.1.

Table 1.1   Windows Character Codes for Special Characters in Western European Languages

FRENCH

À	Alt+0192	à	Alt+0224	Î	Alt+0206	î	Alt+0238
Â	Alt+0194	â	Alt+0226	Ï	Alt+0207	ï	Alt+0239
Ç	Alt+0199	ç	Alt+0231	Ô	Alt+0212	ô	Alt+0244
É	Alt+0201	é	Alt+0233	Œ	Alt+0140	œ	Alt+0156
È	Alt+0200	è	Alt+0232	Ù	Alt+0217	ù	Alt+0249
Ê	Alt+0202	ê	Alt+0234	Û	Alt+0219	û	Alt+0251
Ë	Alt+0203	ë	Alt+0235	Ü	Alt+0220	ü	Alt+0252

GERMAN

Ä	Alt+0196	ä	Alt+0228	Ü	Alt+0220	ü	Alt+0252
Ö	Alt+0214	ö	Alt+0246	ß	Ctrl+Alt+S		

ITALIAN

À	Alt+0192	à	Alt+0224	Í	Alt+0205	í	Alt+0237
É	Alt+0201	é	Alt+0233	Ò	Alt+0210	ò	Alt+0242
È	Alt+0200	è	Alt+0232	Ó	Alt+0211	ó	Alt+0243
Ì	Alt+0204	ì	Alt+0236	Ù	Alt+0217	ù	Alt+0249
Î	Alt+0206	î	Alt+0238	Ú	Alt+0218	ú	Alt+0250

PORTUGUESE

Á	Alt+0193	á	Alt+0225	Í	Alt+0205	í	Alt+0237
À	Alt+0192	à	Alt+0224	Ï	Alt+0207	ï	Alt+0239
Ã	Alt+0195	ã	Alt+0227	Ó	Alt+0211	ó	Alt+0243
Â	Alt+0194	â	Alt+0226	Ò	Alt+0210	ò	Alt+0242
Ç	Alt+0199	ç	Alt+0231	Õ	Alt+0213	õ	Alt+0245
É	Alt+0201	é	Alt+0233	Ô	Alt+0212	ô	Alt+0244
È	Alt+0200	è	Alt+0232	Ú	Alt+0218	ú	Alt+0250
Ê	Alt+0202	ê	Alt+0234	Ù	Alt+0217	ù	Alt+0249
Ì	Alt+0204	ì	Alt+0236	Ü	Alt+0220	ü	Alt+0252

SCANDINAVIAN LANGUAGES (DANISH, NORWEGIAN, AND SWEDISH)

Å	Alt+0197	å	Alt+0229	Ö	Alt+0214	ö	Alt+0246
Ä	Alt+0196	ä	Alt+0228	Ø	Alt+0216	ø	Alt+0248
Æ	Alt+0198	æ	Alt+0230				

Continues

Table 1.1 Windows Character Codes for Special Characters in Western European Languages *(Continued)*

SPANISH							
Á	Alt+0193	á	Alt+0225	Ó	Alt+0211	ó	Alt+0243
É	Alt+0201	é	Alt+0233	Ú	Alt+0218	ú	Alt+0250
Í	Alt+0205	í	Alt+0237	Ü	Alt+0220	ü	Alt+0252
Ñ	Alt+0209	ñ	Alt+0241	¿	Ctrl+Alt+/	¡	Ctrl+Alt+1
OTHER CHARACTERS							
«	Ctrl+Alt+[	»	Ctrl+Alt+]				

Foreign Character Basics: Mac OS

The Mac OS already has an accessory similar to 3-D Keyboard for Windows built in: *Key Caps*, which is found under the Apple menu.

Key Caps, shown in Figure 1.2, displays the characters you get by typing particular key combinations. Press the Shift key, and it shows you uppercase letters. Press the Option key, and it shows you the characters you get when you type letters in combination with the Option key.

Some characters, such as the German letter *Eszett* (*ß*) (also known as a *scharfes S* in Austria and some parts of Germany) have their own unique key combinations, but for diacritics such as accent marks that can appear over a number of letters, you press a series of keys in combination (the keys, like the Option key, which don't actually produce a

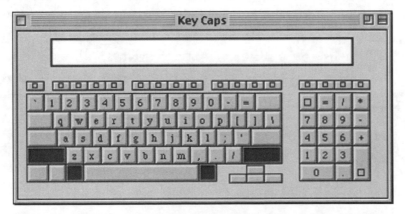

Figure 1.2 The Mac OS Key Caps accessory shows which characters are produced by which key combinations.

character are sometimes called *dead keys*). For example, to put an acute accent (´) over a particular letter, you type Option-e and then the letter. To type the letter *e* with an acute accent (é), you type Option-e, then e. To type the letter *a* with an acute accent (á), you type Option-e, then a. Combinations for other diacritics are shown in Table 1.2.

These key combinations do not vary from one Mac OS application to another. A complete listing of the key combinations required for the special characters of Western European languages is provided in Table 1.3.

As an alternative, third-party shareware solutions such as *PopChar Pro* (www.unisoft.co.at/products/popchar.html) can display a window with the entire character set for a given font and allow you to enter characters into your documents by clicking them in the PopChar window.

Typing the Euro and Other International Currency Symbols

The *euro*, the new unit of currency that 11 of the 15 nations in the European Union began to introduce on January 4, 1999—and for which bills and coins are scheduled to come into circulation in 2001—presents a problem for some computer users. Some can't yet type its symbol, which looks like a letter *e* with an extra horizontal line, as shown in Figure 1.3.

Fortunately, this is relatively easy to fix. Both Microsoft and Apple have already added the euro symbol to fonts that ship with Windows 98 and Mac OS 8.5. Microsoft, Adobe, Monotype, and others have also created freely downloadable fonts which include the euro symbol.

For more information and downloadable fonts, see Web sites from the following companies and organizations:

Table 1.2   Mac OS Key Combinations for Common Diacritics

CHARACTER	KEY COMBINATION
Acute accent (´)	Option-e
Grave accent (`)	Option-`
Diaeresis (¨)	Option-u
Circumflex (ˆ)	Option-i
Tilde (˜)	Option-n

Table 1.3 Mac OS Key Combinations for Special Characters in Western European Languages

FRENCH			
À	Option-`, Shift-a	à	Option-`, a
Â	Option-i, Shift-a	â	Option-i, a
Ç	Shift-Option-c	ç	Option-c
É	Option-e, Shift-e	é	Option-e, e
È	Option-`, Shift-e	è	Option-`, e
Ê	Option-i, Shift-e	ê	Option-i, e
Ë	Option-u, Shift-e	ë	Option-u, e
Î	Option-i, Shift-i	î	Option-i, i
Ï	Option-u, Shift-i	ï	Option-u, i
Ô	Option-i, Shift-o	ô	Option-i, o
Œ	Shift-Option-q	œ	Option-q
Ù	Option-`, Shift-u	ù	Option-`, u
Û	Option-i, Shift-u	û	Option-i, u
Ü	Option-u, Shift-u	ü	Option-u, u

GERMAN			
Ä	Option-u, Shift-a	ä	Option-u, a
Ö	Option-u, Shift-o	ö	Option-u, o
Ü	Option-u, Shift-u	ü	Option-u, u
ß	Option-s		

ITALIAN			
À	Option-`, Shift-a	à	Option-`, a
É	Option-e, Shift-e	é	Option-e, e
È	Option-`, Shift-e	è	Option-`, e
Ì	Option-`, Shift-i	ì	Option-`, i
Î	Option-i, Shift-i	î	Option-i, i
Í	Option-e, Shift-i	í	Option-e, i
Ò	Option-`, Shift-o	ò	Option-`, o
Ó	Option-e, Shift-o	ó	Option-e, o
Ù	Option-`, Shift-u	ù	Option-`, u
Ú	Option-e, Shift-u	ú	Option-e, u

PORTUGUESE			
Á	Option-e, Shift-a	á	Option-e, a
À	Option-`, Shift-a	à	Option-`, a

Continues

Table 1.3 (Continued)

PORTUGUESE			
Ã	Option-n, Shift-a	ã	Option-n, a
Â	Option-i, Shift-a	â	Option-i, a
Ç	Shift-Option-c	ç	Option-c
É	Option-e, Shift-e	é	Option-e, e
È	Option-`, Shift-e	è	Option-`, e
Ê	Option-i, Shift-e	ê	Option-i, e
Ì	Option-`, Shift-i	ì	Option-`, i
Í	Option-e, Shift-i	í	Option-e, i
Ï	Option-u, Shift-i	ï	Option-u, i
Ó	Option-e, Shift-o	ó	Option-e, o
Ò	Option-`, Shift-o	ò	Option-`, o
Õ	Option-n, Shift-o	õ	Option-n, o
Ô	Option-i, Shift-o	ô	Option-i, o
Ú	Option-e, Shift-u	ú	Option-e, u
Ù	Option-`, Shift-u	ù	Option-`, u
Ü	Option-u, Shift-u	ü	Option-u, u
SCANDINAVIAN LANGUAGES (DANISH, NORWEGIAN, AND SWEDISH)			
Å	Shift-Option-a	å	Option-a
Ä	Option-u, Shift-a	ä	Option-u, a
Æ	Shift-Option-'	æ	Option-'
Ö	Option-u, Shift-o	ö	Option-u, o
Ø	Shift-Option-o	ø	Option-o
SPANISH			
Á	Option-e, Shift-a	á	Option-e, a
É	Option-e, Shift-e	é	Option-e, e
Í	Option-e, Shift-i	í	Option-e, i
Ñ	Option-n, Shift-n	ñ	Option-n, Shift-n
Ó	Option-e, Shift-o	ó	Option-e, o
Ú	Option-e, Shift-u	ú	Option-e, u
Ü	Option-u, Shift-u	ü	Option-u, u
¿	Shift-Option-/	¡	Option-1
OTHER CHARACTERS			
«	Option-\	»	Shift-Option-\

Figure 1.3 The euro symbol.

Adobe. www.adobe.com/type/eurofont.htm

Apple. http://developer.apple.com/technotes/tn/tn1140.html

European Union. http://europa.eu.int/euro/html/entry.html

Microsoft. www.microsoft.com/typography/faq/faq12.htm

Monotype Typography. www.monotype.com/html/oem/
euro%5Ffont/download.html

It is also possible to add the euro symbol to your existing fonts with a product called *EuroFonter* from Pyrus N.A. (www.pyrus.com). See Chapter 7 for more information.

To type the euro symbol in Windows, type Alt+0128; on the Mac, Shift-Option-2. To type the symbol for Japanese yen (¥) in Windows, type Alt+0165; on the Mac, Option-y. For British pounds (£) in Windows, type Alt+0163; on the Mac, Option-3.

NOTE
There is an error in the Windows 98 Character Map utility, which Microsoft says it will fix in a forthcoming "service pack." The key combination Ctrl+2 does not produce the euro symbol; Alt+0128 does.

For most other currencies it's generally possible to "cheat" by simply typing an abbreviation, but if you want the real symbols used for your naira, sheqels, and cruzeiros, you'll probably need to get a font designed for the language of the country whose currency you are working in. For more information about custom fonts, see Chapter 7.

Keyboard Layouts

For inputting more than just a few special characters—and for users who are used to native keyboard arrangements that make these characters easier to type—you may want to use a different keyboard layout.

This doesn't mean an actual *physical* keyboard, but rather a software keyboard that determines which keys produce which characters. The standard U.S. keyboard layout is set up to match the keys on a U.S.

keyboard, but there is no reason that this can't be changed. This is what different keyboard layouts do.

For example, on French keyboards, the position of the letters *q* and *a* are switched, the *w* and *z* are switched, and characters such as *é, è, ç, à*, and *ù* are placed for convenient typing without needing to press combinations of keys. Instead of a QWERTY keyboard (named for the first six letters on a standard U.S. keyboard), this keyboard is called *AZERTY*.

Similarly, German has a keyboard called *QWERTZ*, for its switch of the letters *y* and *z*. This is also the same principle behind the Dvorak keyboard, which some people use for better typing efficiency.

Let the User Choose Keyboard Layouts

The fact that many languages have more than one possible keyboard layout means that users should be able to choose their own layouts. The differences between one layout and another may be quite significant. For example, Russian users may be used to the layout used on Russian typewriters, but they may also be accustomed to one of several layouts that map Cyrillic characters to their approximate phonetic equivalents on a U.S. English keyboard. Just providing any keyboard layout for one particular language won't do much good if it's not one that the user knows how to use.

Keyboards are independent of content and do not behave like fonts or formatting. Once text is input, no indication remains of what keyboard layout was used to type it. In other words, with fonts and formatting, if you insert your cursor in the middle of an italicized word in the font Courier, whatever you type will be in italic Courier. But if you insert your cursor in the middle of a sentence typed in the French AZERTY keyboard, you might not be typing in French AZERTY unless you deliberately choose this keyboard. You'll know there is a problem if the wrong letters appear when you type. For example, if you think you are using French AZERTY but are not, you'll keep getting the letter *q* when you really want an *a*.

It is possible to get an actual physical alternative to the standard U.S. keyboard. You can buy these in the countries where the keyboards are used most often, but if a trip abroad isn't in the works, there are options for ordering alternative keyboards. CEL Tech Services (www .celtech.net) makes keyboards (for IBMs only, not PC clones) for a variety of languages. They require no additional software, just a switch of the default keyboard in Windows. Several dozen other options (for PCs and Macs) are also available through California-based World Language Resources (www.worldlanguage.com), and Fingertip Software (www .fingertipsoft.com) sells sets of keytop labels for labeling an existing keyboard, plus a variety of physical keyboards (mostly for PCs).

Windows Keyboards

The *Keyboard Properties* control panel in Windows 98 provides access to more than 70 different keyboards. All of these are for European languages that use the Latin alphabet, in addition to a few keyboards for languages that use the Cyrillic alphabet, such as Russian and Bulgarian. (For information on other languages, such as Japanese, see the last section in this chapter, *Computing Support for Other World Languages and Language Groups*.)

The Keyboard Properties control panel, shown in Figure 1.4, gives the option of adding any of these keyboards to your system by installing them from the Windows 98 CD. Some languages have more than one keyboard option (Spanish has more than a dozen, for the various nations of Latin America), and some keyboards have different options available by clicking the Properties button, such as the option of using a Dvorak key layout in the U.S. keyboard.

When you have installed all the new keyboards you want, be sure to check the "Enable indicator on taskbar" check box. This displays the keyboards that you have available on the right side of your taskbar, as shown in Figure 1.5. The current keyboard is designated by a two-letter code, such as *En* for English, and you can choose from a menu of installed keyboards by clicking the keyboard indicator.

A favorite general choice for those who aren't familiar with foreign keyboards but who still need to type characters for Western European languages is the U.S International keyboard. It contains most of the characters you'll need for Western European languages in relatively convenient and intuitive locations. You may want to make the U.S. International keyboard your default keyboard.

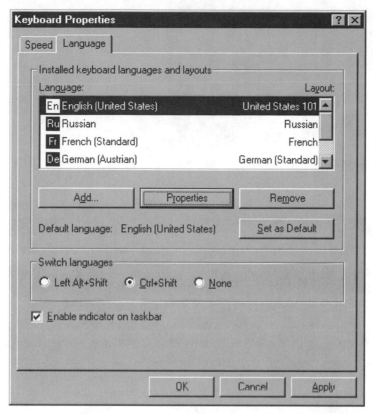

Figure 1.4 The Keyboard Properties control panel in Windows 98.

Mac OS Keyboards

The Mac OS comes with 21 built-in keyboards for languages that use the Latin alphabet. To use them, simply go to the *Keyboard* control panel as shown in Figure 1.6, and select whatever keyboard you need. When more than one is selected, the flag of the current keyboard appears automatically in the upper right corner of the screen near the Applications menu.

You can switch between keyboards by pulling down the Keyboard menu, as shown in Figure 1.7, or you can select Options to set up key combinations for choosing from among the available keyboards. The default key combination for doing this is Command-Space.

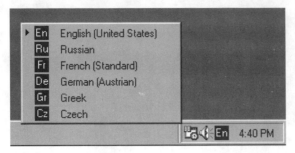

Figure 1.5 The keyboard indicator on the taskbar.

Mac OS 8.5 doesn't include as many keyboard options as Windows 98, but all the major Western European languages are covered. Freeware and shareware options are generally available for the rest. In addition, while Windows 98 includes support only for languages that use the Latin and Cyrillic alphabets, Mac OS 8.5 includes limited built-in support for the major Asian and Middle Eastern languages. For more information, see the last section of this chapter, *Computing Support for Other World Languages and Language Groups.*

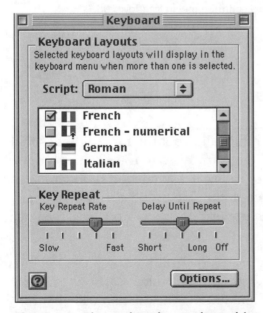

Figure 1.6 The Keyboard control panel in Mac OS.

Figure 1.7 The Keyboard pulldown menu in Mac OS.

Fonts

If you aren't already familiar with font installation in Windows, see Windows Help. On the Mac OS, fonts are installed by simply dragging and dropping them into the System Folder.

For languages with writing systems similar to English—those that read left to right, have alphabets with only a few dozen letters, and so forth—simply installing a font, keyboard layout, and a System script will be enough to allow you to create documents in that language. Czech, for example, has several characters not found in the extended ASCII character set, but simply adding a Czech font, keyboard layout, and script is all that is needed to begin working in Czech.

For fonts that are not included with your system, one source of fonts is Linguist's Software (www.linguistsoftware.com), which sells fonts that can be used with more than 365 languages. Fonts are available for Windows and Macintosh, and in some cases for DOS, Unix, OS/2, NeXT, and other operating systems as well. Other commercial sources of fonts include Ecological Linguistics (P.O. Box 15156, Washington, DC 20003, 202-546-5862); Monotype (www.monotype.com), which creates modules of fonts and scripts for a customer's required language support; FontWorld (www.fontworld.com); and Adobe (www.adobe.com).

There are also many freeware and shareware sources of fonts. A good place to start looking is the Web site for the Yamada Language Center at the University of Oregon, which maintains a thorough catalog of freely downloadable fonts (mostly for the Macintosh) at http://babel .uoregon.edu/yamada/fonts.html. Another list of links to downloadable fonts (some free, some for a fee) with more Windows options is the Fonts in Cyberspace page, maintained by the Summer Institute of Linguistics at www.sil.org/computing/fonts/index.htm.

Buying a font works well for individual work—for example, the word processing of documents that will be printed and distributed on paper—but many fonts are copyrighted and cannot be freely distributed. For sharing multilingual information with others who may not have the same fonts that you do—or who may not be able to use them because they are on another platform—see Chapter 3 and Chapters 9 through 11.

Other languages, however, have features that are difficult or impossible for applications designed for the Latin alphabet to handle. Hebrew, for example, is written from right to left. In Arabic, the appearance of characters varies depending on their position within words. Chinese has thousands of characters, and no simple keyboard-layout rearrangement allows you to type them all.

Advice for working in these languages is provided by language or major language group in the following section.

Computing Support for Other World Languages and Language Groups

When you need to go beyond the languages that originated in Western Europe, you will generally need to install additional software. The way to do this depends on the platform you are using. Although Microsoft is reportedly making significant moves to offer better multilingual support in Windows 2000, at the present time, Apple and Microsoft differ in their approach to multilingual issues.

Apple

Apple's approach has been to make it relatively easy and convenient to get multilingual support for one or more languages, and to be able to use them singly or in combination with one another on any version of the Mac OS (English, French, Hebrew, and so forth).

Apple's support for non-Latin alphabets is based on a technology called *WorldScript*, which allows software developers to easily add multilingual capabilities to their applications, such as the ability to enter text from right to left. These capabilities are made available to

users through a family of language kits (www.apple.com/macos/
multilingual/languagekits.html). More than one language kit can be
installed on the same computer, as shown in Figure 1.8, which enables
support for truly multilingual documents. Each kit comes with a variety of keyboard layouts and transparent labels to attach to your actual
physical keyboard, as well as an assortment of TrueType, PostScript,
and bitmapped fonts.

Apple has been faulted for deviations from accepted standards for
some languages—Apple's Czech fonts, for example, do not use an
encoding called *Latin 2* that has been established for Eastern European

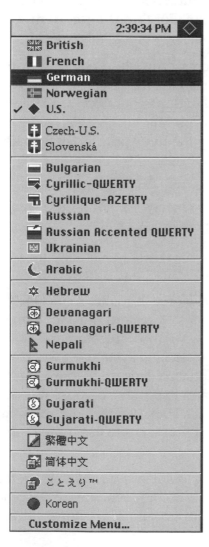

Figure 1.8 Apple's WorldScript technology supports dozens of languages on the same computer.

languages by the International Organization for Standardization (ISO)—but applications are now frequently written in a way that takes care of conversions from one encoding scheme to another. The conversion takes place behind the scenes, and the user may not even be aware of the issue. More information is available in Chapter 3.

Apple also provides significant built-in language support in the Mac OS for the Internet though a feature called *Multilingual Internet Access*. Apple first included Multilingual Internet Access on the Mac OS 8.5 CD, which lets you install support for viewing languages that use the following writing systems: Arabic, Indian (Devanagari, Gujarati, and Gurmukhi), Hebrew, Japanese, Korean, and Chinese (simplified and traditional). Input support is also included for all of these languages except Chinese, Japanese, and Korean. For these, it is currently necessary to buy the full Chinese, Japanese, or Korean language kits.

To install Multililingual Internet Access, run Mac OS Install from the Mac OS CD, and when prompted, choose Add/Remove and scroll down the list of options to Multilingual Internet Access. To view languages that use non-Latin alphabets on Macs running an older version of the Mac OS, it is necessary to buy the full Apple language kits for those languages in order to get support.

For additional information about multilingual support from Apple, see also the links at www.apple.com/macos/multilingual/webinfo .html for Mac-oriented language-specific advice.

Microsoft

Microsoft offers built-in support for more languages in its U.S. version of Windows (namely for the languages of Eastern Europe) than Apple does in the Mac OS, but beyond this, Microsoft recommends using localized versions of the Windows operating system for work in languages that do not use the Latin alphabet. This is an approach that can be cumbersome, time-consuming, and expensive because it is necessary to track down, install, and switch back and forth between multiple language versions of Windows if you want to use more than one non-Latin language on your computer.

Although Microsoft discourages the use of language layers on top of the operating system (warning that their independent development has tended to fragment language support), there are nonetheless a variety of third-party solutions, some of which offer all-in-one language functionality similar to that of Apple's language kits. Details are provided in the following sections. The advice given for the languages covered in this chapter is cross-platform, unless specified otherwise. Not all languages are included, but as much detail as possible is given for the world's major languages and language groups.

Availability

Software companies generally sell the localized versions of their products only in the countries they have been localized for. In other words, you won't have much luck trying to get a localized Japanese version of Windows directly from Microsoft (or mainline PC software vendors) unless you buy it in Japan, and although Apple's family of language kits is available worldwide, Apple officially sells localized versions of the Mac OS only in the countries they were created for.

This doesn't mean that these localized products are impossible to get elsewhere. Whenever possible, options for obtaining them outside of the countries for which they were produced are listed. Most are available through third-party vendors who specialize in international products.

Fonts for the languages discussed in the following sections (and many others) are available from companies including Adobe (www.adobe

One Byte or Two?

Reading about multilingual computing issues, you may come across references to *one-byte* and *two-byte languages*. One-byte languages are languages that contain fewer than 256 characters, which means that they can be represented by 8 bits, or 1 byte. English, German, and Russian are examples of one-byte languages.

Two-byte languages require 2 bytes of memory, which allows for as many as 65,536 characters. This accommodates most of the world's languages, but when a language has thousands of characters instead of dozens, it becomes more complex to handle.

Two-byte languages may also have more than one script. Japanese, for example, uses two phonetic scripts (kana) with more than 160 unique characters in each, as well as an ideographic script (kanji) with thousands of characters. Phonetic scripts describe pronunciation, whereas in ideographic scripts, each character has a specific meaning.

.com), Ecological Linguistics (ecoling@aol.com), Linguists Software (www.linguistsoftware.com), and Monotype (www.monotype.com).

African Languages

Except for Arabic (see the *Middle Eastern Languages* section later in this chapter) and Amharic (the national language of Ethiopia), most of the languages of Africa are written in variants of the Latin alphabet. This makes their use on computers relatively easy, since it is only necessary to install fonts that include special characters and keyboards for ease of input.

The font *TransRoman*, available from Linguists Software (www .linguistsoftware.com), has the characters needed for more than two dozen African languages, including Afrikaans, Ashanti, Masai, Swahili, and Yoruba. The font *AfroRoman*, also from Linguists Software, has characters needed for some of the same African languages, in addition to others, such as Hausa. Both are available for Windows and the Mac OS.

An Afrikaans keyboard is included on the Windows 98 CD.

Tips for Avoiding Trouble

With more and more options built into operating systems and applications for working in other languages—or several languages at once—it can be tempting to install all the language support that is available, so that every one of your machines is ready to work in nearly any language. For machines that are used by more than one person, this would allow input or viewing in any language the user desires.

This may not be as good an idea as it sounds at first.

Most of the time, you can get away with installing support for multiple languages and writing systems on the same computer without any problems. But to be on the safe side, remove (or better yet, don't install in the first place) support for any language you don't need. It's a good bet that quality-assurance testing of, say, Arabic and Chinese support running side by side hasn't been as thorough as for most other elements of your system. Truly baffling conflicts can arise and cause problems such as control panels appearing in other languages, or printers spewing forth the wrong alphabet.

This doesn't mean that it's necessary to segregate languages, but keeping your language-support options as simple as possible will help avoid needless conflicts.

East Asian Languages

All three of the major East Asian languages (Chinese, Japanese, and Korean) have complex writing systems with thousands of characters, requiring special input methods.

Support for all three of the major East Asian languages, plus other languages, is offered in one Windows product that allows you to view and work in all three: *WinMASS 2000*, from Singapore-based Star+Globe Technologies (www.starglobe.com.sg). WinMASS 2000 lets you add these capabilities to off-the-shelf applications within the English Windows environment. A similar Windows product called *AsianSuite* is available from UnionWay (www.unionway.com).

Windows support for Traditional and Simplified Chinese, Japanese, and Korean—including both display capabilities and input method editors (IMEs)—is also available through a well-regarded product called *NJStar Communicator* (www.njstar.com), as well as Microsoft's freely downloadable *Global IME* (www.microsoft.com/windows/ie/features/ime.asp).

Because of similarities in writing systems, in some cases it is also possible to use support for one language to work in another. For example, some Chinese and Korean input options also provide limited support for entering Japanese.

Generally, however, it is necessary to get separate support for each individual language. Use of a Japanese operating system for Chinese work, for example, can cause trouble when printing because characters get mapped to Japanese-encoding equivalents, which means you don't get the characters on paper that you were expecting. "People do need to be careful about what they combine on their computers, since the results are often unpredictable," says Laurel Mittenthal, foreign language computing specialist for the Faculty of Arts and Sciences Computer Services at Harvard University.

The main options for individual East Asian language support are described in the following sections.

Chinese

To support the Chinese language's thousands of characters, it is frequently necessary to distinguish between support for the Traditional and Simplified Chinese script. The Simplified script is the result of an effort that began in the 1950s to simplify the complex Chinese writing system—some Traditional characters require as many as 33 strokes to write by hand. All Chinese characters are drawn to fit within an invisible square frame.

Today, Simplified Chinese is generally used in the People's Republic of China and Singapore, while Traditional is used in Taiwan and by Chinese communities in other countries.

When Chinese is written out in the Latin alphabet, the system of Romanization most commonly used today is called *pinyin*.

Dialects of Chinese such as Mandarin and Cantonese use the same writing system and are written identically, even though in speech they are not mutually intelligible.

Windows

Traditional and Simplified Chinese versions of the Windows operating system itself can be purchased through AsiaSoft (www.asiasoft.com) and World Language Resources (www.worldlanguage.com). Versions of products in Chinese are generally designated with the letter *C* after the name, or *CS* for Chinese Simplified or *CT* for Chinese Traditional, as in Microsoft Windows 98CT.

Support for Chinese in English versions of Windows is available through *Chinese Partner* from TwinBridge (www.twinbridge.com). Chinese Partner provides support to Windows 95 and 98 and Unicode-compliant applications, and includes several traditional and simplified fonts, in addition to eight Unified Chinese fonts which include both the Simplified and Traditional Chinese character sets. Chinese Partner also supports several input methods and can convert to and from several Chinese encoding standards, such as GB, Big Five, GBK, Big Five Plus, and Unicode.

Another Chinese option for Windows is *Chinese Star* from SunTendy America (www.suntendyusa.com), which support Windows 3.x and higher and Windows NT.

Yet another Chinese input option is Motorola's *Wisdom Pen* (www.mot.com/MIMS/lexicus), a Chinese handwriting-recognition system that transforms characters written with a stylus on a pressure-sensitive tablet to digital characters.

Mac OS

Simplified and Traditional Chinese versions of the Mac OS itself can be purchased from AsiaSoft (www.asiasoft.com) and World Language Resources (www.worldlanguage.com).

Other versions of Mac OS 8.5 (including U.S. English) include display-only support for Chinese Web browsing through the Multilingual Internet Access option, which can be installed from the Mac OS 8.5 CD.

Apple's *Chinese Language Kit* (www.apple.com/macos/multilingual/chinese.html) provides support for Simplified and Traditional characters, with six fonts and a variety of input methods, including Pinyin, Zhuyin, and Cangjie. Character entry is made easier by automatic prompts for the most likely phrases beginning with the last character you have entered. You can also enter characters through handwriting or voice with the Apple *Advanced Chinese Input Suite* (www.asia.apple.com/datasheets/as/acis.html), which must be purchased separately.

Some users have expressed concerns about the Chinese Language Kit's inability to convert to and from certain encoding schemes, but generally the kit gets high marks.

The Chinese Language Kit displays the menus of localized applications in Chinese and also allows you to work with Chinese in other applications that support Apple's WorldScript technology. Documentation is in English and Chinese.

Getting Localized Apple OSs and Language Kits

One way to get updates of language kits and localized versions of the Mac OS is by subscribing to the *Apple Developer Connection Mailing* (developer.apple.com/programs/mailing.html). The monthly CD includes software updates, including many of interest to multilingual users, as they become available.

The entire family of Apple's language kits is also bundled with the multilingual publishing application *Ready, Set, Go! Global*, detailed in Chapter 10, "Multilingual Publishing, Graphic Design, and Multimedia."

Japanese

Japanese writing uses three scripts, kanji, hiragana, and katakana, in addition to a widely used Latinization called *romaji*. Kanji is based on Chinese ideographic characters, while kana (hiragana and katakana) is syllabic. It is common to write in a mix of both kana and kanji.

Windows

Japanese versions of the Windows operating system itself can be purchased through AsiaSoft (www.asiasoft.com) and World Language Resources (www.worldlanguage.com). Versions of products in Japanese are generally designated with the letter *J* after the name, as in Microsoft Windows 98J.

One of the main options for Japanese support in English versions of Windows is Pacific Software Publishing's *KanjiKit 97* (www.pspinc .com/lsg). KanjiKit 97 is a Japanese utility for English versions of Windows that allows you to use the Internet and email in Japanese with Netscape or Internet Explorer, and to use Japanese in the English versions of Microsoft Word, Excel, and other Unicode-compliant applications.). KanjiKit 97 includes the Katana FEP (front-end processor, an input method), plus Mincho and GothicTrueType fonts. An additional font pack is also available. KanjiKit 97 runs on Windows 3.x or higher and Windows NT. A 15-day trial version can be downloaded from Pacific Software Publishing's site.

Another source of Japanese support in English versions of Windows is *Japanese Partner*, from TwinBridge (www.twinbridge.com). Japanese Partner allows you to work with Japanese characters (kanji and kana) in the standard English Windows environment, and a variety of input methods are included. The basic version includes four Japanese fonts, and an extended version offers 15 additional fonts and full compatibility with Microsoft Office.

J-Text Pro 1.1 from NeocorTech (www.neocor.com) is a basic $39 Japanese word processor for Windows 95/98 and NT. J-Text Pro lacks the full features of a standard word processor like Microsoft Word, but it allows basic word processing in Japanese because it comes with its own fonts and front-end processor for entering Japanese characters. Some reviewers say the J-Text input method for Japanese characters takes some getting used to, but one of J-Text's advantages is that it requires no additional support.

Mac OS

The Japanese version of the Mac OS itself can be purchased from AsiaSoft (www.asiasoft.com) and World Language Resources (www .worldlanguage.com). Versions of products in Japanese are generally designated with the letter *J* after the name, as in Mac OS 8.5J.

Other versions of Mac OS 8.5 (including U.S. English) include display-only support for Japanese Web browsing through the Multilingual Internet Access option, which can be installed from the OS 8.5 CD.

Apple's full *Japanese Language Kit* (www.apple.com/macos/ multilingual/japanese.html), which can be installed with any language version of the Mac OS in addition to other language kits, includes the Kotoeri input method, along with three kanji fonts and a Roman and kana keyboard layout. When the kit is installed, applications that have been localized for Japan will display Japanese menu bars. Documentation is in English and Japanese.

The kit handles Japanese text well but does not by itself allow you to type text vertically. The kit can be used with applications supported by Apple's localized Japanese system as well as with English applications that support Apple's WorldScript technology, such as the word processor Nisus Writer.

Korean

Korean writing consists of two scripts, Hangul and Hanja. *Hanja* refers to Chinese ideographic characters, while *Hangul* is an alphabet consisting of 10 vowels and 14 consonants that was invented for Korean 500 years ago but not widely accepted until the twentieth century. It is possible for Hanja and Hangul characters to be used in the same text.

Windows

Korean versions of the Windows operating system can be purchased through AsiaSoft (www.asiasoft.com) and World Language Resources (www.worldlanguage.com). Versions of products in Korean are generally designated with the letter *K* after the name, as in Microsoft Windows NT 4.0K Workstation.

One of the main options for Korean support in English versions of Windows is *Korean Partner*, from TwinBridge (www.twinbridge.com). Korean Partner includes four TrueType Korean fonts, an electronic

Korean dictionary, and a code converter and font editor. Korean Partner is available for Windows 3.x and higher.

Another option is Union Way's *Hangul Pro Pack* (www.unionway.com), which allows you to read and input Korean characters in the standard English Windows environment, including Microsoft Office, Publisher, WinFax Pro, and other applications. Hangul Pro Pack is available for Windows 3.x and higher.

Mac OS

The localized Korean version of the Mac OS can be purchased from AsiaSoft (www.asiasoft.com) and World Language Resources (www.worldlanguage.com). Versions of products in Korean are generally designated with the letter *K* after the name, as in Mac OS 8.5K.

Other versions of Mac OS 8.5 (including U.S. English) include display-only support for Web browsing in Korean through the Multilingual Internet Access option, which can be installed from the OS 8.5 CD.

The full *Korean Language Kit* (www.apple.com/macos/multilingual/korean.html) supports both Hangul and Hanja and can also display the menus of applications in English or Korean if they are designed for this possibility. It includes two keyboard layouts for native speakers and two romaja modes for easy Korean input by nonnative speakers.

The Korean Language Kit also includes the Hanja Dictionary Utility, which allows a user to create a personal Hanja dictionary. The kit includes five Korean TrueType fonts that include more than 2,000 symbols and 4,888 Hanja characters, as well as an extended symbol character set and support for Japanese hiragana and katakana characters. Documentation is in English and Korean.

A Korean font package with 27 fonts for Macintosh is available from World Zusson (www.worldzusson.com).

Eastern European Languages

Many of the languages of Eastern Europe (including Czech, Polish, and Rumanian) use modified versions of the Latin alphabet, and so basic support generally requires only a font and keyboard layout. Things are more complicated, however, for languages including Russian, Bulgarian, Serbian, and Macedonian (and some of the non-Slavic languages of the former Soviet Union, such as Uzbek and Kazakh, although many of these languages are returning to their original writing systems), which all use the Cyrillic alphabet and therefore require Cyrillic fonts and keyboard layouts.

Support for the Cyrillic alphabet is also complicated by several competing standards, including Windows Cyrillic, Unicode, and the Russian KOI8 (for Code of Information Exchange) standards. In addition, not every Cyrillic font contains all the characters needed for every language that uses the Cyrillic alphabet, so you may need to use fonts designed specifically for the languages you are working in. For more details, including information on support for other operating systems, see the Russify Everything page at www.siber.com/sib/russify.

Windows

The Windows 98 CD includes support both for Eastern European languages that are based on the Latin alphabet as well as for those that use Cyrillic. However, some of these keyboard layouts lack *phonetic* options that may be very helpful to non-native typists.

Sources of additional support, such as keyboard layouts, converters, fonts and proofreading tools, include the *Cyrillic Starter Kit* and *Central European Starter Kit*, both from Fingertip Software (www.cyrillic.com). Links to additional sources of keyboard layouts, coding converters, and other tools and advice is provided through a page maintained by Paul Gorodyansky, at http://ourworld.compuserve.com/homepages/Paul_Gorodyansky.

Fully localized versions of Windows for Russian and other Eastern European languages are available from (www.worldlanguage.com).

Mac OS

Mac OS support for Eastern European languages that use the Latin alphabet is available from commercial providers of fonts, or sometimes as shareware and freeware. Common sources for these fonts are the localized versions of Mac OS 7.0.1 that Apple makes available by FTP from ftp://ftp.info.apple.com/Apple_Support_Area.

For languages such as Russian and Bulgarian, which use the Cyrillic alphabet, it is necessary to get a copy of Apple's *Cyrillic Language Kit* (www.apple.com/macos/multilingual/cyrillic.html), which includes support for Russian, Ukrainian, Bulgarian, Belorussian, Macedonian, and Serbian. Several TrueType fonts are included, as are keyboard layouts for typists familiar with native Russian keyboards and those who are using Latin keyboards.

Fonts in Apple's Cyrillic Language Kit lack accented vowels, but these can be added with shareware fonts such as Nevsky (ftp://ftp.brown .edu/pub/language_lab/Nevsky.sea.bin). For additional details about Russian, see the Russification of the Macintosh page at http://solar.rtd .utk.edu/partners/rusmac.

Can't Find What You're Looking For?

Email discussion lists and other Internet-based resources exist for many of the world's languages, and these can be a great place to find out more about the computing issues that arise in one language or another. One source is the Internet Resources for Language Teachers and Learners page, maintained by the University of Hull in Britain at www.hull.ac.uk/cti/langsite.htm, or the Human Languages Page at www.june29.com/HLP. Links to other online resources are also available through www.indigo.ie/egt/langlist.html, and The Yamada Language Center at the University of Oregon, which maintains a catalog of these lists at babel.uoregon.edu/yamada/lists.html.

Both Microsoft and Apple generally keep their overseas offices separate from operations in the United States, but for times when it may help to go straight to the source, a complete listing of Microsoft's overseas offices is available at www.microsoft.com/worldwide, and for Apple at www.apple.com.

Indian Languages

Indian languages use many writing systems, several of which may be used in the same country. The government of India, for example, makes official use of 12 different writing systems.

Devanagari is used by languages such as Hindi, Marathi, and Nepali (as well as Sanskrit, from which they descended). Devanagari has 52 basic symbols and is written from left to right. Devanagari also has its own set of symbols for numerals, but today Arabic numbers are typically used.

Gujarati is used for the languages Gujarati and Kacchi, has 51 basic characters, and is written from left to right. Gurmukhi, used by the Panjabi language, has 55 characters and is also written from left to right. Mayalam has 50 characters, is written left to right, and is used by languages including Tamil and Telugu.

A Perso-Arabic script is used for Urdu, the official language of Pakistan. See the *Middle Eastern Languages* section later in this chapter for more information.

The diversity of Indian languages has led to a lack of standardization, but the main options are detailed. For additional information about Hindi in particular, see the Hindi Language Resources site at www.cs .colostate.edu/~malaiya/hindilinks.html.

Windows

Although support for Tamil, Hindi, and other Indian languages that use Devanagari script is planned for Windows 2000, Microsoft and third-party support for these languages has generally been limited. One option is the *Indian Language Keyboard Program* from AC Zone (www.aczone.com/ilkeyb) for Windows 3.1 and higher and Windows NT, which provides fonts and support for Indian scripts such as Devanagari, Gujarati, and Mayalam. Another option is to use software such as *OnePen* (www.zem.co.uk/mlsoft/onepen.htm), which allows you to insert non-Latin characters in most Windows applications.

Fonts for Indian writing systems and individual Indian languages are available from Monotype (www.monotype.com) and Ecological Linguistics (email: ecoling@aol.com).

Mac OS

Apple's *Indian Language Kit* (www.apple.com/macos/multilingual/ indian.html) provides support for languages written in the Devanagari, Gujarati, and Gurmukhi writing systems. It can also be used to view Indian Standard Code for Information Interchange (ISCII)-compatible Indian language sites on the Web, and includes the default INSCRIPT keyboard layout, as well as a phonetic Latinized option for input on a QWERTY keyboard. The kit includes three TrueType Indian fonts, along with matching English typefaces.

Middle Eastern Languages

Two of the major Middle Eastern languages, Arabic and Hebrew, have special requirements because they are bidirectional languages and require both right-to-left and left-to-right input.

Arabic

Arabic's writing system of 28 letters is written from right to left and is a cursive script in which most letters connect with the letters next to them. There are no block letters, nor is there any distinction between upper- and lower-case. However, each letter can have up to four forms (initial, medial, final, and separate) depending on its context, and unlike the rest of Arabic writing, numbers and other mathematical expressions are written from left to right.

Windows

Localized Arabic versions of the Windows operating system can be purchased from the AramediA Group (aramedia.com) or World Language Resources (www.worldlanguage.com). Two versions ship on the same CD, enabled and localized. The *enabled* version supports Arabic text in an English environment, while in the *localized* version, the entire user interface is in Arabic. Both fully support the Arabic language and the Hijri calendar, which is based on lunar cycles.

An Arabic text-to-speech option called *Reading Machine* is available from Sakhr Software (www.sakhrsoft.com).

Mac OS

Apple's *Arabic Language Kit* (www.apple.com/macos/multilingual/ arabicfarsi.html) includes support for Arabic and Persian, including seven Arabic fonts and six Persian fonts. It also supports the Hijri (lunar) calendar. The kit basically supports Urdu and other languages that use the Arabic writing system, although it lacks characters and diacritics for some of these languages. In these cases, it may be necessary to modify an existing Arabic font with Fontographer (see Chapter 7) or to buy third-party pan-Arabic fonts.

Hebrew

Like Arabic, to which it is related, Hebrew is a bidirectional language. Text is written from right to left, but numbers and mathematical expressions are written left to right as in English. Hebrew script has 22 letters, 5 of which have two shapes depending on their position within words. The Hebrew writing system is also used for languages such as Yiddish.

Windows

Hebrew versions of the Windows operating system can be purchased from World Language Resources (www.worldlanguage.com). Two versions ship on the same CD, enabled and localized. The *enabled* version supports Hebrew text in an English environment, while in the *localized* version, the entire user interface is in Hebrew.

Mac OS

Apple's *Hebrew Language Kit* (www.apple.com/macos/multilingual/hebrew.html) includes support for Hebrew and Yiddish, with six fonts for Hebrew with Yiddish characters and various keyboard options, including a QWERTY keyboard. The kit does not support cantillation marks (for musical recitation) and therefore may not be appropriate for religious texts.

Turkish

The Windows 98 CD includes support for Turkish, which uses a modified version of the Latin alphabet. A selection of Turkish fonts for the Mac OS is available at the Multilingual Macintosh Support page at www.indigo.ie/egt/earra_bog/apple/index.html, or http://babel.uoregon.edu/FontLayout/FontMain.html, as well as from commercial font vendors.

Other Languages

The following languages do not fit easily into any of the language groups discussed above. Nonetheless, their use with computers requires some explanation.

Esperanto

This artificial language uses a modified version of the Latin alphabet. For fonts, check www.homunculus.com/babel/Fonts/EspFonts.html and http://babel.uoregon.edu/yamada/fonts/esperanto.html.

Greek (Modern)

Greek is written from left to right and requires no special support other than fonts and keyboard layouts. Fonts, however, may be monotonic—referring to a reform made in the 1980s to make Greek writing conform to a single accent—or the traditional polytonic.

Fonts and keyboards for Greek are included on the Windows 98 CD. For support on the Mac OS, try the Multilingual Macintosh Support page at www.indigo.ie/egt/earra_bog/apple/index.html, or babel .uoregon.edu/yamada/fonts/greek.html.

Pacific Languages

The font *TransRoman*, available from Linguists Software (www .linguistsoftware.com), has the characters needed for major Polynesian languages such as Fijian and Samoan, as well as Hawaiian. Windows support for Maori (spoken in New Zealand) is available from Reddfish (www.reddfish.co.nz/reddfish/kete.htm).

For More Information

For information about these and additional languages, an excellent source is the *WorldType Solutions Catalogue* from Monotype (www.monotype.com), which provides font samples of the company's type offerings for more than two dozen writing systems. More than this, however, the informative catalog is also a great primer on the world's languages.

Next

After setting up your system for multilingual work, you'll also need applications that can handle various languages. These are discussed in the next chapter.

2

World-Savvy Applications

After you've installed support for the languages you need to work in, you might think you're ready to begin working. You might not be. It's possible that you'll still need to make sure that your applications can support the languages you need to work in.

Nearly all applications are capable of working with the languages that use the Latin alphabet, mainly because these languages are processed in basically the same way. But for work in languages with more complex writing systems—those with thousands of characters, or right-to-left input—you need to make sure that your applications can handle the language's special requirements. And even if you are working only in languages that use the Latin alphabet (French, German, Swahili, and so forth) you may need to make sure that your applications can hyphenate, sort, or alphabetize them correctly. You might also want spell-checking dictionaries and other tools and references.

This chapter discusses the world-readiness of the major applications in three main categories: productivity applications, Web browsers, and databases. Information about *optical character recognition* (OCR) applications for scanning texts created in languages other than English is also included.

Email applications are discussed in Chapter 9, "Multilingual Electronic Communication." Sending and receiving email that is written in languages other than English is a particularly complex topic, because email requires not only display capabilities, but also the ability to input a language in a response.

Features of the applications discussed in this chapter will naturally change (especially in the fast-paced competition among Web browsers), but an explanation of the basic multilingual features available today is offered based on what is currently available, and what may become available in the future.

NOTE

Many of the applications mentioned in this chapter support Unicode, an international character set that is coming into more widespread acceptance. Unicode is described in more detail in Chapter 3, "Multilingual Compatibility Issues," but basically, any application that supports Unicode today is likely to be well-positioned for multilingual use in the future.

Localized Applications

For the best possible support of the language you need to work in, you may want to use a version of an application that has been localized for your language and which includes custom support for that language's writing system. Since support for the most complex writing systems is still spotty (or nonexistent) in some English applications, getting a localized version may be your only option.

Many localized versions of applications are designated with an abbreviation for the language after the name of the application. Adobe Illustrator 7.0J, for instance, is simply the Japanese version of this graphics program.

Many software vendors do not sell localized versions of their software outside of the countries for which they have been localized. Among other things, technical support for localized versions can be a headache for them, and they may not be able to provide you with support if you are using a localized version of a product outside of the country it was localized for. You can still buy localized versions through third-party software vendors, such as World Language Resources (www.worldlanguages.com), but you may have to rely on yourself—or call overseas—for tech support.

Word Processors and Office Suites

This section describes several productivity applications—especially word processors—that are able to handle multilingual documents.

Microsoft Office

Historically, Microsoft's productivity applications in the Office suite (www.microsoft.com/office) have come up short for multilingual users. For example, Microsoft Word for the Mac still lacks full support for Apple's WorldScript technology, the most widely used way of handling complex writing systems on the Mac.

Things are changing, however, and Microsoft has caught up in a big way. Microsoft Office 2000, which was designed with multinational organizations and multilingual work in mind, supports Unicode (as does Office 98 for the Mac) and allows work in more than 80 languages.

Office 2000 has an impressive array of multilingual features, including automatic language detection (which can automatically switch to the correct language for spelling and grammar checking in more than 30 languages), and support for writing and editing multiple languages. This includes support for complex writing systems, such as languages written from right to left, like Arabic and Hebrew (system-level support through a localized version of Windows may be required). Office 2000 allows you to specify language-sorting options and look up words in a thesaurus of another language, and it can convert between Traditional and Simplified Chinese characters or between Hangul and Hanja in Korean. It also provides the long-awaited ability to change the language of the user interface itself with a simple setting, as shown in Figure 2.1.

It's impossible to provide exact details on all of Office 2000's many multilingual features, but extensive documentation is provided by the Office 2000 Help system. Within Office 2000, doing a Help search on the word *language* brings up detailed instructions on how to use dozens of the suite's language features. It may also be helpful to simply read through the Help section "About multilingual features in Office."

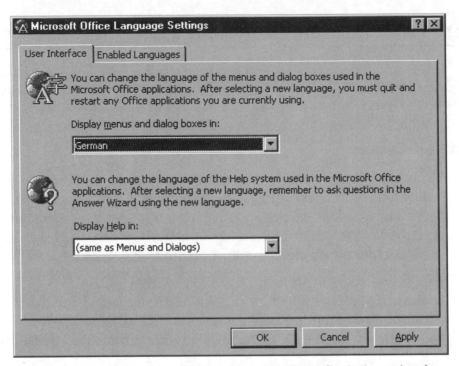

Figure 2.1 Office 2000 allows you to easily change the application's user interface.

Microsoft calls Office 2000 the "first truly global desktop applications suite" because it uses a single code base, instead of the previous 36 localized versions that had to be administered and deployed as separate applications. With these capabilities—especially in combination with the multilingual capabilities slated for Windows 2000 (see Chapter 3)—Office 2000 is well suited for multilingual work in a large organizational environment.

Office 2000 has, however, been criticized for its large size and its limits based on operating-system-level language support. Any version of Windows can support European languages, but complete display and input support for Asian and bidirectional languages requires localized versions of Windows itself, or Windows 2000, which merges together language support that was previously available only through localized versions. Some users also express disappointment with Office 2000's limits on ways to switch between input methods for languages such as Chinese. They prefer smaller, more flexible applications, such as some of the other options listed later in this section.

The most recent Mac version of Microsoft Office, Office 98, supports Unicode, although it does not fully support Apple's WorldScript technology. Office 98 does support some WorldScript application program interfaces (APIs), such as the APIs that keep fonts and the keyboards needed to type them in sync.

Where the installed system supports it, Office 98 also makes sure that any localized Office version can display documents created in any other localized version. Where cross-platform fonts are available, it allows documents to display and print the same on Windows versions of Office as on the Mac. Office has its own code and mapping tables that take Unicode characters stored in Office documents to display them under the local operating system, and vice versa.

Other language details about Office: The localized Japanese version of Office supports vertical text entry. Arabic and Hebrew versions of Office 98 are not available. The Office 98 Value Pak Proofing Tools provide spelling and grammar-checking tools for nine languages.

Users of older versions of Microsoft Word (such as Word 97 for Windows or Word 6 for the Mac) that did not include built-in proofing tools for other Western and Eastern European languages can buy them from Alki Software (www.proofing.com).

Sort Order

The problem of how to sort tables and databases with information in other languages is complicated by the fact that there are several ways to sort some languages. Chinese and some other Asian languages, for example, can be sorted phonetically, by stroke order, or by other methods.

Sorting in languages that use the Latin alphabet is relatively easy. The sorts basically work the same as in English, except that allowances must be made for characters such as the French ç.

In the Mac OS, sort order can be set in the Text control panel, which gives you a choice of different behaviors for different scripts. For the Roman (Latin) script, for example, you can choose among "behaviors" that include English, French, Italian, and Norwegian. Similar options are added when you install support for languages that don't use the Latin alphabet.

In Windows, sort order cannot be set globally the way it can under the Mac OS, but some individual applications provide sorting options for different languages. See the documentation for the applications you use for more details.

Corel WordPerfect Office 2000

Corel WordPerfect Office, the flagship product of Ottawa-based Corel (www.corel.com), has some multilingual features of its own, mostly in the form of proofing tools.

The Corel WordPerfect Language Module, which is sold separately from WordPerfect for a suggested retail price of $49.99, supplies multilingual writing tools in various combinations for 29 languages. The module provides spell-checking, thesaurus, grammar-checking, and hyphenation capabilities, as well as language-specific fonts.

The complete set of writing tools is available for French, Spanish, Dutch, German, and Italian, while another 24 languages, such as Afrikaans, Danish, and Russian, have only some of the tools. Except for the major Western European languages, many have only PC options available. The WordPerfect Language Module supports versions of WordPerfect as far back as version 5.1 for DOS and version 3.5 for Macintosh.

ClarisWorks/AppleWorks

Apple's office suite AppleWorks (www.apple.com/appleworks) was formerly known as ClarisWorks. Claris was a subsidiary that has since been reabsorbed by Apple.

AppleWorks is available for both the Mac OS and Windows, and it has a loyal following among multilingual users thanks to its longtime support of Apple's WorldScript technology. Trial versions of AppleWorks for both Mac and Windows are available for download from Apple's site.

With the installation of proper language support—either through Apple's family of language kits (see Chapter 1, "The World-Ready Computer") or Multilingual Internet Access in Mac OS 8.5 and higher, which includes full language support for several languages—the AppleWorks word processor can handle multiple languages and writing systems in the same document. Other word processors such as Nisus Writer (discussed next) have similar capabilities, but AppleWorks shines when it comes to multilingual spreadsheets and database files. In a spreadsheet, for instance, it is possible for each cell to contain data written in another language or writing system. For instance, one cell could be written left to right in French, the one next to it right to left in Hebrew, and the one next to that in Chinese.

Through AppleWorks' preferences, it is also possible to set default fonts to accompany the use of different language scripts (for instance, your favorite Chinese font for whenever you write in Chinese), and different language sorting options.

Nisus Writer

Nisus Writer, from Nisus Software (www.nisus.com), is a Mac-only word processor whose multilingual capabilities have long surpassed those of Microsoft Word, making it a favorite among Mac users. Nisus Writer has full WorldScript support, meaning that it can handle nearly any language. Nisus can also import and export Word and WordPerfect files, and Nisus is said to be planning a Windows version of Nisus Writer.

Nisus Writer's strengths include speed and low memory requirements, unlimited undos, noncontiguous selection, and a table and equation editor. Unfortunately, however, Nisus Writer's equation editor cannot handle double-byte text (2 bytes are required to represent languages such as Chinese or Japanese which have thousands of characters). Equations in languages such as Korean have to be handled within the word processor itself, or you can use the application's graphics layer to draw them. Nisus can support vertical text (for languages such as Japanese) with additional tools.

A free download of Nisus Writer version 4 (an earlier release) is available from the Nisus site, where you can also download 30-day trial copies of the latest version.

Universal Word

Universal Word, from the WYSIWIG Corporation (www.wysiwig.com), is a Windows-only multilingual word processor sold to support specific language groups, or to support all languages. The application's multilingual features include a simple pulldown menu for switching languages (see Figure 2.2), search-and-replace capabilities to and from multiple languages, multilingual mail merge, a built-in keyboard display, and the ability to toggle between languages with an icon.

Figure 2.2 The language menu in Universal Word.

Global Writer

Global Writer, from Unitype, Inc. (www.unitype.com), is a Windows word processor that supports more than 80 languages. Although criticized for the absence of features found in other word processors, such as support for macros and footnotes, Global Writer has multilingual strengths, such as its own built-in front-end processors (input methods), meaning that third-party support is not required to work in languages such as Korean, Chinese, or Japanese.

Unitype also offers a new product called *Global Office*, which serves as a multilingual front-end processor for Microsoft Office. Global Office provides support for more than 100 languages, including Chinese, Japanese, Korean, and the right-to-left languages, and includes a variety of keyboard layouts.

Lotus SmartSuite

The applications of Lotus SmartSuite (www.lotus.com) allow you to install language support by installing additional copies of the application localized for the language you need. The first language installed becomes your default language.

Lotus SmartSuite does not presently support Unicode.

WorldWriter

WorldWriter is a word processor from Blue Shoe Technologies (www.blueshoe.com/fraindex.htm) that supports 39 languages and includes OCR and translation capabilities for Chinese.

Other Applications

In addition to the applications already discussed, there are other productivity applications available for particular languages or particular language groups. For more information, see the Web sites for these products:

Ichitaro (www.justsystem.co.jp/index_e.html). A Japanese word processor.

iLeap (www.indolink.com/iLEAP). A word processor for Indian languages.

NJStar (www.nistar.com). A word processor for Chinese and Japanese.

WordMage (www.lavasoft.com). A Japanese word processor, Web page editor and browser, and study aid.

Additional Proofing Tools

Additional language support, such as tools for hyphenation or specialized vocabularies, is also available:

Circle Noetic Services (www.mv.com/ipusers/noetic). Makes hyphenation packages, spell checkers, and other tools.

Routledge Technical Dictionaries (www.routledge-ny.com). Produces technical dictionaries on CD-ROM for French, German, and Spanish.

MediaLingua (www.medialingua.com). Offers Multilex, a family of electronic dictionaries for English, German, French, Spanish, Italian, and Russian.

Bilingual versus Multilingual

Thanks to the widespread use of the Latin alphabet throughout the world, most productivity applications—even those localized for languages such as Japanese—can handle English and other Latin-alphabet languages as well. They are bilingual in the sense that they support two different writing systems. If truly multilingual support is important to you, however, look for the support of several different writing systems, as offered by some of the applications discussed in this chapter. Individual localized versions of applications may not have all the multilingual capabilities you need.

Web Browsers

Initially limited to only the Latin alphabet (and even then imperfectly, as soon as diacritics for languages other than English became involved), Web browsers have made dramatic strides over the last few years in their ability to correctly display texts in other languages. Both Microsoft Internet Explorer and Netscape Navigator include built-in options for browsing languages that don't use the Latin alphabet, and companies like Microsoft and Apple have created software that makes it easier for users of their operating systems worldwide to browse the World Wide Web.

This section contains an overview of language support in the major browsers, plus details about a few other choices.

The applications discussed here have the ability to display pages written in other languages, but they can't translate them to English or another language for you. For more information on translation options, see Chapter 8, "Translation and Localization."

Information about forms and other interactive Web features that may

Localized Browsers

The makers of the most popular Web browsers have translated the user interfaces for their products into several languages. If you want a version other than English, check to see what other language options are available for your platform when you download browsers and browser updates. Not every language is available, but the major European languages and Japanese are usually available.

require input methods for languages with complex writing systems are discussed in Chapter 9.

Microsoft Internet Explorer

Microsoft Internet Explorer has two main multilingual features: adjustable language preferences and a choice of character sets and fonts. Localized versions are available in several languages.

Web pages in languages other than English can be created with a variety of different character sets. When dealing with pages that have not been coded properly, viewing a page created in one of these character sets requires knowing which set was used so you can select it manually in your browser. It is possible, however, for Web pages to include a CHARSET metatag that identifies which character set is needed to view a particular page. Current versions of Internet Explorer can read this metatag and automatically switch to the character set that displays the page correctly.

In Figure 2.3, a Web page in Czech (not shown) that was tagged for the Windows 1250 character set allowed Internet Explorer to automatically switch to this Windows character set—even though this page was viewed on a Mac.

If a particular page fails to display correctly, you can manually choose another character set with this submenu to find one that works. See Appendix A for more information about which character sets are used for which languages. Each time you switch character sets, Internet Explorer refreshes the page.

When you switch to another page that has no CHARSET metatag (as many pages written in English do not), you may find that this page displays in the font of the last page that did specify its metatag. You may need to switch back manually.

You can also set default languages, character sets, and fonts in Internet Explorer's Internet Options (Preferences on the Mac OS). The Fonts option, as shown in Figure 2.4, allows you to select a default character set as well as proportional and fixed-width fonts.

The Language option, shown in Figure 2.5, allows you to select a default language for sites that can send pages in your choice of several languages. Some sites make their content available in more than one language.

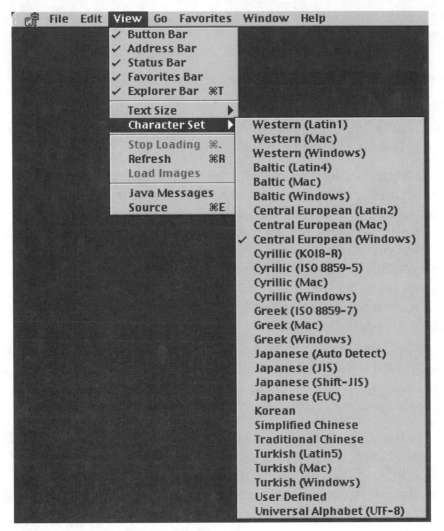

Figure 2.3 Internet Explorer can choose the correct character set for some pages automatically.

Freely downloadable support for other languages can be added to Internet Explorer through Windows Update. To connect, go through Windows Update at the top of the Windows Start menu, or connect directly to http://windowsupdate.microsoft.com. For the Mac OS, use the Multilingual Internet Access capabilities that are included on the CD-ROM for OS 8.5 and higher.

Currently, Internet Explorer for Windows has more options for default languages than Internet Explorer Mac OS version 4.5, which is limited

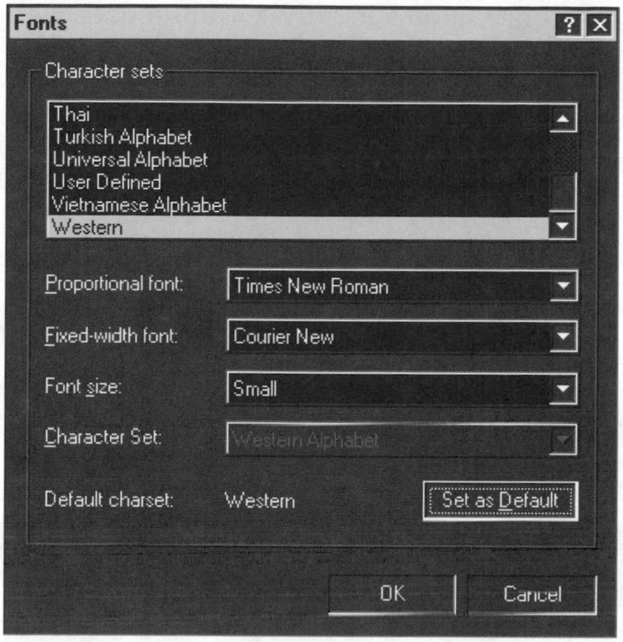

Figure 2.4 The Fonts option in Internet Explorer.

to English, German, Spanish, French, Italian, Japanese, Korean, Portuguese, Swedish, and Chinese. This doesn't mean that other languages are impossible to view, but simply that the application's ability to automatically show you a site in the language of your choice is more limited.

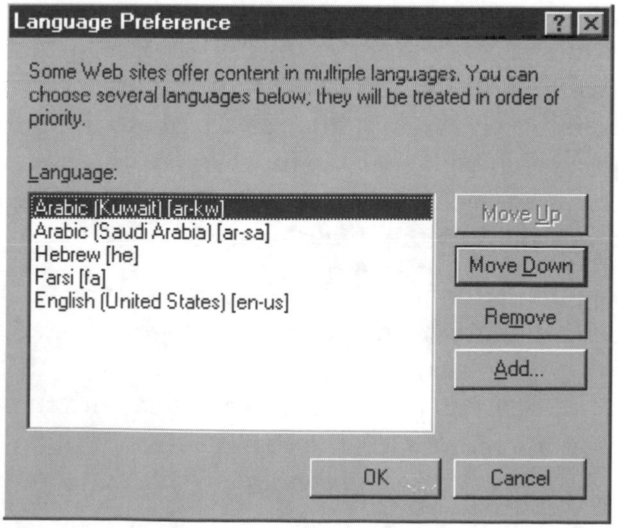

Figure 2.5 The Language option in Internet Explorer.

For more background information about the multilingual capabilities of Internet Explorer, see Microsoft's One Browser, Many Languages page (www.microsoft.com/windows/ie_intl/sl/homeuser/archive/b7lang3.htm).

Language-Specific Web Searches

The AltaVista search service (www.altavista.com) offers a capability of special interest to multilingual users: the ability to search by language.

Using the Language pulldown menu, you can specify that you want to search only for documents written in a particular language. Select Russian and search for *Moskva* (the Latinization of Moscow) and your search results will include only pages in Russian. With proper input support (see Chapter 9 for more information) you can also enter searches in non-Latin writing systems if the search engine supports them.

You can also create a custom home page with your own language preferences by going to the Set Your Preferences option at the bottom of the AltaVista home page.

Netscape Navigator

Netscape Navigator offers essentially the same multilingual capabilities as Internet Explorer. You can specify which language you would like to view a page in if the page's creator has made different language options available, and you can choose which character sets you would like to use to view pages if Navigator doesn't choose the correct character set for you. Currently, the only significant difference is that Macintosh versions of Netscape Navigator are less adept at automatically switching to the correct character set than Internet Explorer. Sometimes selecting the right character set manually doesn't work either, even for pages that Internet Explorer handles well.

Language options in Navigator are set through the Preferences submenu. In the Preferences window, the Fonts subcategory (listed under Appearance) gives you a choice of character sets (referred to in Navigator as *encodings*) and the fonts you would like to use with those character sets. As shown in Figure 2.6, the Languages submenu (under Navigator) lets you set your order of preference when versions of a Web page in more than one language are available.

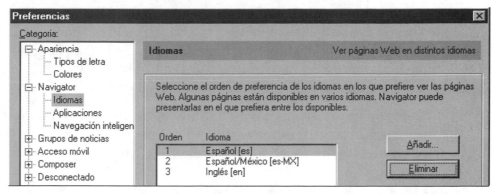

Figure 2.6 Adding language-viewing preferences in a localized Spanish version of Netscape Navigator.

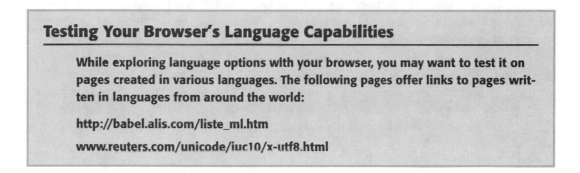

Testing Your Browser's Language Capabilities

While exploring language options with your browser, you may want to test it on pages created in various languages. The following pages offer links to pages written in languages from around the world:

http://babel.alis.com/liste_ml.htm

www.reuters.com/unicode/iuc10/x-utf8.html

Netscape maintains a Netscape International page at http://home.netscape.com/menu/intl with detailed information about how to use the browser with languages other than English.

Tango

Both Microsoft Internet Explorer and Netscape Navigator do a reasonable job of displaying Web content in languages other than English, but at times their language capabilities seem to have been added on almost as an afterthought. Tango, from Alis Technologies (www.alis.com), is a browser that was designed from the start with multilingual users in mind. Tango is currently available for Windows 3.1, Windows 95/98, and Windows NT. A company spokeswoman said that Alis has no plans to support other platforms such as Linux or Mac OS.

Unlike the most popular browsers, you have to pay for Tango, but the $60 suggested retail price gets you a variety of multilingual features not found in other browsers. As shown in Figure 2.7, Tango allows you to choose the language of its user interface as a Preference (19 choices are available), and control over character sets and other language features is provided through buttons on Tango's button bar. A 30-day demo version can be downloaded or ordered on CD.

Even more impressive is Tango's ability to handle language input in more than 90 languages for email and online interactive forms. These capabilities are discussed in more detail in Chapter 9.

Server-Based Support for Multilingual Browsing

If you're stuck at a terminal that doesn't have a multilingual-capable browser but you need to access a page created in another language, try the Multilingual-HTML Browser (http://mhtml.ulis.ac.jp). Through a form on this page, you can enter the URL you are trying to view, choose a character set to view it in, and then the MHTML server will display it for you.

This is nothing like using a properly equipped multilingual browser of your own (the results can be crude), but if you're working at a machine that doesn't have a world-savvy browser installed, MHTML might be just what you need.

Databases

A lack of multilingual capabilities can be a drawback for any application, but the problem can be particularly significant in databases. Documents such as reports or letters might be read by only a handful of people, all of whom probably share a common language because they

Figure 2.7 Tango lets you switch the language of your user interface.

work together. Databases can be much more complicated. A single database might be accessed by hundreds of people throughout an organization. These people might be on different continents and speak several different languages. Not only may they need multilingual applications, but the format of the data they access may have to support multiple writing systems. If this need doesn't exist now, it may in the future, and it can be difficult to add multilingual support as an afterthought.

The database applications discussed here are principally desktop databases. Considerations for enterprisewide information-management systems are discussed in Chapter 5, "Strategies for Multilingual Development and Globalization." Language details about network-database solutions such as Microsoft SQL Server and Oracle 8 are provided in Chapter 11, "Creating Multilingual Internet and Intranet Sites."

Access 2000

Access 2000 was the only application in the Office suite to change its file format from Office 97. The change was to accommodate Unicode support. As part of the Office 2000 Suite (described earlier in this chapter), Access has a variety of multilingual features, including support for more than 80 languages and the use of the same code-base, regardless of which localized version of the product you are using.

FileMaker Pro

FileMaker Pro—produced by FileMaker, Inc. (www.filemaker.com), formerly Claris Corporation—originated on the Macintosh but is available for Windows as well. FileMaker Pro's support for non-Latin alphabets and writing systems is currently somewhat limited.

FileMaker Pro does not support right-to-left text processing, and although English versions of FileMaker can correctly display data entered in languages such as Japanese (including vertical text) if the proper fonts are installed, full support for entering data in the major East Asian languages is available only in localized versions of File-Maker for Chinese, Japanese, and Korean. Files from these localized versions cannot be fully supported by the U.S. English version. File-Maker Pro has been localized into more than 35 languages.

Starting with version 4.0, FileMaker Pro corrects a problem previously experienced by users of non-U.S. English versions of Windows who use international characters in file names, which resulted in incorrect finding and sorting within files that used these languages. FileMaker Pro 4.0 alters the registry file in international versions of Windows to allow the indexing of international characters.

FileMaker also makes available the cross-platform Language Dictionary CD, which provides spell-checking for Afrikaans, Catalan, U.S. English, U.K. English, Danish, Dutch, Finnish, French, German, Italian, Norwegian, Portuguese, Brazilian Portuguese, Spanish, Swedish, and Swiss German.

Lotus Approach

As a part of the Lotus SmartSuite (previously described), the relational database Lotus Approach can support other languages by installing additional versions of the application that have been localized for a particular language. The first language installed becomes the default language.

Personal Oracle8 Multiple Language Edition

Personal Oracle8 Multiple Language Edition (www.oracle.com/support/products/po8/nt95/html/index.html) is a desktop version of the enterprise-level Oracle8 database. The multiple language edition requires Windows 9x or NT and supports 30 languages.

OCR Software

The advantages of optical character recognition (OCR) software can be particularly important in multilingual work. Accurate OCR usually beats retyping a document—even if a few corrections have to be made by hand—and the advantage can be even greater if you're dealing with a document written in a language that may be cumbersome to type on a keyboard not designed for that language. The key combinations used to type diacritics, and the other input methods used to enter double-byte languages like Japanese, almost inevitably slow a typist down.

Dozens of off-the-shelf OCR choices exist. It isn't possible to review them all here, but the multilingual features of several of the most popular OCR packages are listed. When choosing an OCR package for multilingual use, it is naturally important to make sure that it supports the language or languages that you use, but also that it can handle more than one of these languages in the same document if necessary. Many OCR applications include or offer the ability to recognize and work with several of the most common languages that use the Latin alphabet.

When choosing, it's also a good idea to check which languages for dictionaries and spell-checking are included, and whether localized versions of the user interface are available. Naturally, you'll also need to look at features independent of language, such as the application's overall capabilities, the scanners and formats it supports, and so forth.

The following applications—all of which have some multilingual capabilities—were among the top scorers in a *PC Magazine* survey of OCR software in 1998.

Cuneiform OCR

Cuneiform OCR, from Cognitive Technology (www.ocr.com/html/cunei30.html), is available for Windows 3.1 and higher and Windows NT. Dictionaries and built-in spelling checkers are available for English, German, French, Italian, Spanish, Portuguese, Dutch, Danish, Swedish, and other languages, and Cuneiform for Russian offers OCR support for the Cyrillic alphabet. In addition, you can purchase Cuneiform with the choice of user interface and manuals in one of four different languages: English, French, German, or Russian.

OmniPage Pro

OmniPage Pro, from Caere Corporation (www.caere.com), is available for Windows and the Mac OS. It recognizes 13 languages: U.S. English, International English, Danish, Dutch, Finnish, French, German, Italian, Norwegian, Portuguese, Brazilian Portuguese, Spanish, and Swedish. In addition, the user interface is available in International English, Spanish, French, Italian, Portuguese, German, Dutch, and Swedish. A localized Japanese version is available as well.

Figure 2.8 shows settings for recognizing more than one language in the same document.

Presto OCR Pro

Presto OCR Pro, from NewSoft (www.newsoft.com.tw/product/ocrpro.html), is available for Windows. Its spelling checker and multilingual dictionaries recognize English, French, and German, or combinations thereof.

Readiris

Readiris, from I.R.I.S. (www.irisusa.com), is well regarded among multilingual users for its ability to recognize 50 Western and Eastern European languages. It is available for Windows and the Mac OS, and a demo version can be downloaded through the company's Web site.

Recognita Plus

Recognita Plus, from the Hungary-based Recognita Corp. (www.recognita.hu), is available for Windows. It can recognize more than 100 languages in multiple combinations. Languages include those

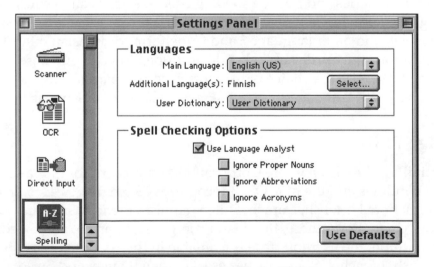

Figure 2.8 OmniPage Pro is an OCR application that allows settings for recognizing more than one language in the same document.

of Western and Eastern Europe, as well as several African, Asian, and Native American languages that use the Latin alphabet.

TextBridge Pro

TextBridge Pro, from ScanSoft (www.xerox.com/scansoft), is available for Windows and the Mac OS. It recognizes English, French, Italian, German, and Spanish. Modules for Brazilian Portuguese, Dutch, Danish, Finnish, Norwegian, and Swedish are also available in a free language pack. TextBridge Pro is also part of a larger scanning suite called *Pagis*.

OCR for Other Non-Latin Alphabets

Most of the OCR applications discussed so far support only the Latin or Cyrillic alphabets, but there are other choices. In addition to OmniPage Pro, which has a localized Japanese version, there are other OCR options, including Kanji OCR from Pacific Software Publishing (www.pspinc.com), and KanjiScan OCR from NeocorTech (www .neocor.com), for Japanese.

OCR support for other languages is limited, but check the online catalog of World Language Resources (www.worldlanguages.com) for current offerings in Arabic, Chinese, Hebrew, and other languages.

Next

Once you have your own system and applications set up for multilingual use, you may still encounter difficulty sharing documents with other multilingual users. These issues are discussed in the next chapter.

CHAPTER 3

Multilingual Compatibility Issues

Setting up your computer with basic language support and selecting applications that will let you work with those languages is necessary, but it may not be sufficient. Language support is complicated by competing standards for individual languages, and Unicode, a truly global standard for multilingual text encoding and communication for all languages, has still not completely taken hold. Unicode itself is still being updated to accommodate additional languages and special characters within languages that have already been encoded.

This chapter describes the Unicode standard, the basics of Unicode support on different computing platforms, and how to share multilingual documents more easily across different platforms.

Unicode

Before looking at the details of the Unicode universal character set, it is helpful to understand what motivated the efforts to establish a truly global standard for handling text.

Keeping Terms Straight

A single *character* can have many glyphs. A *character set* or *encoding* is an ordered collection of characters. A *font* is a collection of glyphs that share the same style.

Other terms that may require clarification include *multilanguage*, *multiscript*, and *multilingual*. Technically, *multilanguage* refers to support for multiple languages that use the same writing system (script) and the same set of attributes, such as sort order. *Multiscript* refers to support for multiple scripts but within the same set of attributes. *Multilingual* refers to support for multiple scripts and multiple attributes.

The Origins of Unicode

More than a hundred different character sets for the world's languages exist, and to make matters worse, some languages have more than one character set in common use. Russian, for example, has a standard called *KOI8* (which in Russian stands for "code of information exchange") that originated in the Soviet Union, but other standards for handling the Cyrillic alphabet were developed independently in the West during the Cold War, when little or no information was being exchanged electronically.

Compatibility may not have been much of an issue then, but it is now. Something was needed to clear through this kind of confusion, and the need for a multilingual standard accelerated in the 1990s with the advent of the World Wide Web.

Unicode originated in the late 1980s in discussions between engineers at Apple and Xerox who wanted to make true multilingual computing easier through a character set that would encompass all the world's languages. Other computer scientists, scholars, national representatives, and interested parties joined their work and created the non-profit Unicode Consortium in 1991, incorporated as Unicode, Inc. The consortium publishes the Unicode standard in book form, *The Unicode Standard: Version 2.0* (Addison-Wesley, 1996).

The Unicode standard is now up to version 2.1, and information about additions since the version 2.0 book was published is available at the consortium's Web site at www.unicode.org (*not* unicode.com, which is the site for a private company). The site also contains code charts, additional scripts and characters under consideration, the first chapter of the published book, and other details.

Unicode Today

Unicode is a universal character set designed to accommodate most of the world's languages, similar to the way in which the extended ASCII character set accommodates the scripts of the languages that originated in Western Europe. But whereas 8-bit extended ASCII has room for only 256 characters, 16-bit Unicode has room for 65,000. Even this number isn't enough for all the characters in all the written languages that have ever existed, but the vast majority of the world's living languages have been included in Unicode. Version 2.1 contains close to 39,000 characters.

The Unicode standard can also be extended in the future as needed with 16 additional planes of 65,000 characters. The current plane is called *Plane 0*, or the basic multilingual plane. "Plane 0 is close to full as far as new character subsets are concerned," says Andrea Vine, an internationalization architect at Sun. Expanding into additional planes "has not yet happened, but the first additions . . . are very close."

It's important to note that compliance with Unicode does not require full Unicode support. A Unicode-compliant font meant to be used with only one language, for example, does not need to contain characters for all of Unicode's other languages, too. Instead, Unicode compliance requires that a font for one language does not interfere with another.

The International Organization for Standardization (ISO) also has a universal character set, known as *ISO 10646*. This is not a competing character set, however, since Unicode and the ISO have been cooperating to ensure consistency. Characters in both character sets are mapped to the same code points, but Unicode specifies additional properties, some of which are discussed in the following sections.

Unicode Characteristics

One of the fundamentals of Unicode is that it is based on characters, not glyphs. A *character* is the smallest component of a written language with its own distinct semantic value, such as the letter *a*. *Glyphs* are different renderings of a character, and a single character can have different glyphs. Figure 3.1 shows different glyphs for the character *a*.

In English, this difference between glyphs and characters is usually just a matter of formatting or style, but it becomes more significant in other languages, such as Arabic, in which characters change shape depending on their position in a word. Different glyphs for the same character must be provided for by the font, and there is not a specific Unicode code point for each individual glyph.

If you need to refer to specific Unicode characters, Unicode character tables are available at http://charts.unicode.org/Unicode.charts/normal/Unicode.html. Unicode code-point values range from 0000 through FFFF in a base-16 *hexadecimal* numbering ranging from 0 to 9 and then A to F for the numbers 10 to 15. The character LATIN SMALL LETTER A, for instance, is number 0041, while THAI CHARACTER FO FAN is number 0E1F.

The primary scripts currently supported by Unicode are Arabic, Armenian, Bengali, Bopomofo, Cyrillic, Devanagari, Georgian, Greek, Gujarati, Gurmukhi, Han, Hangul, Hebrew, Hiragana, Kannada, Katakana, Latin, Lao, Malayalam, Oriya, Tamil, Telugu, Thai, and Tibetan. It is important to note that these scripts generally do not correspond to individual languages. Languages that use the same script share characters, so it is not necessary to duplicate them. This reduces the overall size and complexity of the Unicode character set. For example, English, Spanish, French, German, and dozens of other languages share the characters of the Latin script, and Chinese, Japanese, Korean, and Vietnamese share the ideographic characters of the Han script.

Unicode also encodes numbers, diacritics, punctuation marks, currency, and mathematical and other symbols. Unicode allows for *dynamic composition*, which makes it possible to combine characters, such as a base character like *a* and a diacritic like ` to render the single character *à*. This ability to combine characters also helps cut down on the size and complexity of the character set.

No layout or language data is encoded in Unicode, but Unicode characters do have properties that indicate whether they are numeric,

a a *a* a a   **Figure 3.1** Glyphs for the character *a*.

upper- or lowercase, right-to-left or left-to-right, and so forth, which assists applications that process Unicode text.

There are several ways of encoding the Unicode universal character set (UCS), but the most common—and one which you may see references to when looking into compatibility issues—is UTF-8, which stands for UCS Transformation Format, 8-bit. For technical reasons, Unicode may be expressed (through the application of an algorithm) as other encodings as well, such as UTF-7. UTF-16 is the most straightforward format, since Unicode is 16-bit in its most basic form.

Unicode Fonts and Applications

Unicode can't be directly used as a font-encoding scheme because of its foundation in characters (not glyphs), its lack of formatting information about individual characters, and the fact that it encodes text by scripts and not languages. For these reasons, Unicode fonts—which might best be called *Unicode-conformant fonts*—are fonts that can correctly render Unicode-encoded text, but this conformance does not require covering the entire Unicode character set. You won't be able to type Chinese in a Unicode-conformant Tamil font. Unicode-conformant fonts simply stake out a set of characters—the Latin characters needed for Portuguese, for instance—and then render them on screen or in print in a particular style.

Fonts are available for the entire Unicode character set, which allows you to type or display text in any Unicode-supported writing system. For instance, the font Arial Unicode MS (provided with Microsoft Office 2000) does include characters for all of Unicode's scripts. To install this Windows font from the Microsoft Office 2000 CD if you don't already have it, choose Add or Remove Features, then Office Tools, International Support, and finally Universal Font.

Because a font that can render all 39,000 characters in the Unicode 2.1 standard is extremely large, universal fonts like this should be used appropriately. A database that will contain information from languages that use many different writing systems is one example of a situation in which it might make sense to use a universal font. For work in only a few languages, however, it would be impractical to use a font that includes characters for writing systems which you may never use. It is also important to keep in mind that the typographic characteristics of a universal font—its appearance and subtle glyph differences—

may not be ideal in all locales. Han characters, for example, may be essentially the same, but more traditional forms are used in Taiwan and Korea, more simplified forms are used in Japan, and even more simplified forms are used in China.

Unicode applications are simply applications that can correctly handle documents created using the Unicode text-encoding standard, no matter what language they are written in, as long as the operating system and installed fonts support the characters specific to that language. With Unicode support now becoming standard at the system level, it is a good idea to expect—and require—the applications you use to support Unicode, as well. Unicode is essentially the new ASCII, and in the future, documents not created in Unicode may need to be converted. Worse, they could simply be lost due to incompatibility. For more information about planning for a more multilingual future, see Chapter 5, "Strategies for Multilingual Development and Globalization."

Additions to the Unicode Standard

Unicode was intended to provide a single standard that encompasses all the world's languages, but at this point the Unicode standard is still growing. More languages are being added, and more symbols are occasionally added for languages already included in Unicode. The addition of new characters or glyphs may need to be taken into account.

"There are many reasons for the glyph count rising," says Kamal Mansour, manager of non-Latin products for Monotype, Inc. "There may be addition of ligatures, contextual forms, and so on. People are starting to request finer features such as having alternative shapes for the same character, and for languages such as Japanese where type can be set either horizontally or vertically, there's a need for vertical alternative shapes."

This doesn't mean that the Unicode standard is unstable however, and changes are unlikely to affect your work unless they relate to the language or languages you work in. "There's always a need to add additional minority scripts, and scripts that represent historical languages," said Mansour, "but in terms of commercial usefulness, the standard at the current level is already supporting scripts that cover 99 percent of all commerce."

System-Level Language Support

Chapter 1, "The World-Ready Computer," describes language support in Windows and the Mac OS from the standpoint of the end user: how to type characters in non-Latin alphabets, how to install non-English keyboards, and so forth. To discuss cross-platform compatibility, it's necessary to look more closely at multilingual issues at the system level.

Unicode is the future of text processing, and it becomes especially important for multilingual compatibility across platforms—or even between different applications running on the same platform. This section looks at Unicode support and other multilingual features in current (and forthcoming) versions of Windows and the Mac OS, as well as in BeOS, Linux, OS/2, and Solaris.

Windows

Windows NT was designed from the beginning for international distribution, and it supports Unicode throughout. Windows 98, unfortunately, uses Unicode only for common components that it shares with Windows NT, such as some dynamic link libraries (DLLs), which are small programs that can be called by a larger program when needed. Instead, Windows 98 uses a character-encoding scheme called *double-byte character set* (DBCS).

Things are expected to improve, however, in Windows 2000, the successor to both Windows NT 4.0 and, eventually, Windows 98. Windows 2000 is currently planned in four versions: Windows 2000 Professional (Microsoft's mainstream desktop operating system) and three systems for large businesses and enterprise use (Windows 2000 Server, Windows 2000 Advanced Server, and Windows 2000 Datacenter Server). All four will be based on the core code of what was the Windows NT line, which means full Unicode enabling and greater multilingual capabilities.

"Entering and display of all supported scripts . . . is available on all versions of Windows 2000," says F. Avery Bishop, program manager for Microsoft's Multilingual Developer Communications. "This means that on the base English version, or any other version of Windows 2000, you can type in Arabic, Thai, Hindi, Japanese, Chinese (Simplified and Traditional), Korean, Tamil, and of course, all the European languages . . . assuming the application supports those scripts."

NOTE

Microsoft has announced that delays in the planned migration of Windows 98 to Windows 2000 mean that an interim version of Windows 98 will be released in late 1999 before the mainstream version of Windows 2000 is ready (perhaps not until 2001 or 2002).

Mac OS

Previously relying on language support based on individual scripts (in the form of the Mac OS WorldScript and QuickDraw GX technologies), Apple has been building greater Unicode support into successive versions of the Mac OS. Mac OS 8.5 includes Apple Type Services for Unicode (ATSUI), which fully conforms to the Unicode Standard version 2.1 and is essentially a successor to WorldScript and QuickDraw GX. Mac OS application developers can also take advantage of text encoding converters that handle conversions to and from Unicode, as well as other text encodings.

The next major release of the Mac OS will be Mac OS X (10), scheduled for late 1999.

Other Operating Systems

Though the majority of computer systems run versions of Windows and (to a lesser extent) the Mac OS, there are a number of other operating systems with multilingual capabilities as well. While these operating systems are not discussed in detail in this book, their essential multilingual features are described here.

BeOS (www.be.com). The BeOS supports Unicode and Unicode fonts throughout the system, and uses the encoding format UTF-8 (the same as Java). BeOS utilities, such as BTextView, are multibyte-character-aware, and the BeOS incorporates an input-method architecture available to application developers that provides for the input methods required by languages such as Chinese and Japanese. The Japanese version of BeOS (BeOS-J) ships with a Japanese input method.

Linux (www.linuxresources.com). As with other aspects of the increasingly popular Unix-based operating system Linux, it can be difficult to find details about this open-source software since there is no single, central source of information about it. For example, Web searches about multilingual support in Linux seem to turn up mostly references to support for fictional languages such as Klingon. Linux does, however, support Unicode, and a series of Linux how-to online tutorials about subjects such as how to configure Linux for use with various languages is available at http://metalab.unc.edu/mdw/HOWTO/HOWTO-INDEX-3.html#ss3.1.

OS/2 Warp (www.software.ibm.com/os/warp). Both client and server versions of OS/2 Warp (as well as WorkSpace On-Demand, a network-computing-based client option) have been localized into more than 30 languages. OS/2 Warp input and output are Unicode compliant, and the system supports the exchange of Unicode-compliant multilingual documents with other operating systems. OS/2 Warp Server for ebusiness has been localized for more than a dozen languages (with additional versions supporting other languages, albeit through an English user interface), and also includes a feature called the graphical locale builder, which allows users to modify international dates and other settings more easily.

Solaris (www.sun.com). The Sun Solaris operating environment supports Unicode with a framework that allows for the development of applications for any country or region of the world. Solaris support for Unicode is based on the UTF-8 format.

Sharing Multilingual Documents

With more and more Unicode support in the operating systems and applications we use, sharing multilingual documents should be less and less of a problem. But unless you're already creating documents in Unicode-compliant fonts with Unicode-savvy applications in an OS that supports Unicode—and unless everyone you share documents with does the same—you may have some compatibility issues to think about. Unicode probably will replace most existing language encodings, but it could take years to make this switch, even for the creation of new documents (much less for the conversion of older legacy data that was originally created in a non-Unicode format but which still needs to be accessed).

If you can't yet rely completely on Unicode for sharing multilingual documents, it makes sense to standardize as much as possible. Options for sharing files created by different applications on different platforms, and converting formats from one to another, are getting better, but there's nothing quite as easy as simply avoiding the need to convert in the first place. In the case of sharing multilingual documents, this may not just be a convenience; it may be the only way to avoid some much more difficult conversion problems.

If possible, try to come to an agreement on a standard with those you work and exchange files with. Smooth multilingual document sharing depends on several things: matching system-level support for the encoding schemes you use (for both display and, if necessary, input), matching application support for the encoding schemes you use, and matching fonts. The more you deviate from matching these factors, the more likely you are to have problems.

If you want to exchange files through email, there are additional considerations, because non-ASCII text may be muddled in transit. These issues are discussed in more detail in Chapter 9, "Multilingual Electronic Communication."

It is important to note that language-encoding support is not an all-or-nothing proposition. Using a system that supports Unicode doesn't rule out the use of older encodings. If you need to continue using documents created in older formats—or need to continue sharing files with those who do—you may need to become familiar with using several different encoding schemes, if you aren't already.

For more details about the different encoding schemes used by different languages, see Chapter 1. For details about displaying multilingual content on the Web, see Chapter 11, "Creating Multilingual Internet and Intranet Sites." And for details about converting from one encoding scheme to another—as is, unfortunately, often necessary in a world that still hasn't settled on one worldwide standard—see Chapter 7, "Creating and Converting Multilingual Resources."

Acrobat and DynaDoc

Because support for the Unicode standard is still spotty—and because it can be impossible to arrange for everyone you share documents with electronically to use the same applications, fonts, and system-level language support—it is sometimes helpful to simply avoid the whole issue. For documents that simply need to be viewed, not added to or revised, one good option can be the use of applications such as Adobe Acrobat or DynaLab's DynaDoc, both of which make it possible to exchange multilingual documents in a portable document format that requires only a reader, not matching fonts and other language support.

Adobe Acrobat

Acrobat and the widely used portable document format (PDF) from Adobe (www.adobe.com) can be used to deliver multilingual content to those who don't have matching fonts and language support installed on their systems. PDF documents can be created directly from applications such as Microsoft Office, or by simply dragging and dropping a document onto the Acrobat application.

With any localized language version of Acrobat 4.0 or the free Acrobat Reader, it is possible to view documents containing text in English, French, German, Japanese, Chinese, Korean, Swedish, Spanish, Dutch, Italian, Arabic, Hebrew, and Brazilian Portuguese. For the best language support, use the latest available version of Acrobat Reader.

For the best results, Acrobat makes it possible to embed fonts in a PDF document. This ensures that the document will appear exactly as intended when viewed by other users, and also makes it easier to edit and print PDF files. However, when creating PDF files with embedded Asian fonts, it is important to keep in mind that the more fonts and the more text you use, the larger your document will become. You can prevent your PDF files from becoming prohibitively large by not embedding Asian fonts, but this will require your readers to have them instead. Free Asian fonts (Simplified and Traditional Chinese, Japanese, and Korean) for Acrobat Reader are available from www.adobe.com/prodindex/acrobat/cjkfontpack.html.

DynaDoc Lite

Less well known than Adobe Acrobat is DynaDoc Lite, another portable-document technology from DynaLab Inc. (www.dynalab .com). DynaDoc Lite can embed two-byte fonts in a portable electronic document and preserve the document's original appearance and layout regardless of which fonts, applications, and system the recipient has. Those who want to view them need only the free DynaDoc Reader (Windows and Mac OS) or DynaDoc Lite plug-in for Netscape Navigator or Microsoft Internet Explorer.

DynaDoc Lite documents can be created by other applications through the DynaDoc Lite Generator, which acts like a printer driver and allows you to create DynaDoc Lite portable documents as if you were printing. Instead of getting a paper printout, you get a portable electronic document.

DynaLab specializes in products for the Chinese, Japanese, and Korean markets, and DynaDoc Lite was developed with two-byte text in mind. DynaLab's Web site contains sample Chinese, Japanese, and Korean documents that highlight DynaDoc Lite's strengths.

Next

Having looked at multilingual support and compatibility, there is one other issue that affects many multilingual users: the difficulties that arise when traveling internationally, such as getting technical support or going online. Solutions for these problems are provided in the next chapter.

Language to Go: Keeping Connected While Traveling

Sometimes you not only need to work in more than one language, you may also need to travel to the countries where the languages you work in are spoken. It can be difficult to stay on top of your work when you've left behind the conveniences of your main office: access to the Internet, installation disks and manuals, the desktop computer where you have installed support for multiple languages, and so forth.

This chapter assumes that you don't have a well-established office—or a tech-support staff to help you out—in all the countries you may be visiting for your multilingual work. If you need to be your own tech-support person and arrange your own dial-up Internet access while traveling abroad, this chapter is for you. It offers advice on how to prepare for a trip, get technical help, and stay connected while traveling abroad (service listings in this chapter are not meant to be comprehensive, but merely to suggest options for needs that may arise). Advice about choosing software for learning and reviewing another language is also provided.

Before You Go

Even if you're just traveling in your own country—in fact, even if you're just telecommuting from home—one of the biggest sources of trouble is simple forgetfulness. It's a lot easier to forget one thing than to remember everything, and with multilingual work, there's even more—fonts, keyboards, applications, and so forth—to forget.

The easiest and most foolproof way to avoid this problem is to use the same computer all the time—a *laptop*. Laptops and their screens are becoming almost as powerful and comfortable to use as desktop models, but even if you use a laptop exclusively, you'll need to remember to bring files that you may usually store on disks or external hard drives, or that may be available only through the network in your office. It's basic advice, but it bears repeating: Try to think of everything you could possibly need before you leave. You'll be glad you did when you arrive in Agadir.

If you usually use a desktop computer but switch to a laptop for travel, try to remember all the language support (localized versions of the system, language kits, fonts, keyboards, applications, and so forth) that you have installed to make your desktop system work. See Chapter 1, "The World-Ready Computer," to jog your memory if it's been awhile since you set up your computer.

Utilities like the *Briefcase* in Windows (or the *Synchronize Folders* option in Mac OS) can help you keep track of and update documents that you create, but they will be of limited help in synchronizing the language-support options you may have installed. The only real solution may be to get in the habit of installing any language support you install on your desktop machine on your laptop at the same time. And to stay within the letter of your license, keep in mind that this may mean buying more than one copy of the software you use.

If possible, try to arrange for a way to connect remotely to your organization's internal network, and perhaps even the hard drive of your desktop computer. Various options exist for doing this, but they vary greatly depending on your network and security arrangements. Check on options for doing this before you leave.

If you do forget some critical aspect of your multilingual support, such as a font, and you need to receive multilingual documents, it can help

When All Else Fails . . .

If you get to your destination and find that you've forgotten something really important, such as a localized application, it may help to try to find a local reseller for what you need. Many hardware and software companies make complete lists of their offices worldwide available through their Web sites. For Microsoft, connect to www.microsoft.com and follow the *U.S. & International* link. Similarly, Apple provides links to the sites of its offices around the world at the bottom of the Apple home page, www.apple.com. It may help to check (bring along the URLs if necessary) the Web sites of the companies that make other multilingual software you use. Stopping by their local reseller may let you buy what you're missing, or it might give you the chance to ask questions to solve or work around your problem.

Even if you don't need anything and everything is working fine, it can be worth a trip to the local reseller. They may carry localized versions of operating systems, applications, and other products that are hard to get outside of the country they were designed for.

to have a fax number as a last resort. Receiving faxes through your hotel or a local business center can be one option, but another (which avoids the awkwardness of trying to receive faxes on your fax modem) is to use a service like *JFAX* (www.jfax.com), which allows you to choose a fax number which will automatically convert your faxes to an electronic format and forward them as attachments to the email address of your choice. Local JFAX numbers are available in major cities throughout the United States and in some other countries, as well. With an arrangement like this, you could be seamlessly receiving faxes regardless of where you are in the world, as long as you have access to your email.

Travel Hardware

Unfortunately, getting the software on your laptop set up and bringing all the documents you need is only half the battle. It won't do you much good if you can't plug your computer into the hotel's electrical outlet, or connect it to the phone jack to use a modem. You may run into 10 different kinds of electrical outlets around the world, and 40 different kinds of phone jacks.

Laptops

Before you buy power adapters, it's a good idea to check first whether your laptop can handle the electrical standard of the country or countries that you'll be visiting. Most models are built to handle a range of voltages, but if you have any doubt, check your laptop's technical specifications. The United States runs on a 110-volt alternating current, while much of the rest of the world runs on a 220-volt alternating current.

It's important to remember that simple adapters, which fit over the end of your power plug and allow it to fit into a different kind of outlet, usually do not convert voltage. Your laptop power supply must be rated for the voltage in use in the country you are visiting. In other words, a power supply rated for between 100 and 240 volts can handle voltages within that range without the use of a voltage transformer. Check with your laptop's manuals or manufacturer if you aren't sure. If your laptop can't handle another voltage, you'll need a voltage transformer. Otherwise, your equipment could be destroyed.

Airport metal detectors and X-ray machines should cause no damage to information stored on electronic devices, but the motors that drive the belts on some security machines use magnets that can damage magnetically stored information. To reduce exposure to these magnets, place your laptop as close to the machine's entrance as possible and remove it from the other end as soon as you can. And if caution is worth the inconvenience, have your laptop inspected by hand. Be sure the battery is charged so that it can be turned on to demonstrate that it works (and isn't just being used as a case to smuggle something instead). If possible, keep copies of your most important work on removable storage media and pack these with your checked baggage so that they are not exposed to the same conditions as your carry-on.

For more detailed information about the electrical requirements in countries around the world, check the Web site for *Go-Global.com* (http://go-global.com/Voltage.html) or *American Express* (http://travel .americanexpress.com/travel/docs/resources/tips/electric.shtml).

Phones and Modems

For phones, the U.S. RJ11 phone plug comes closest to being a worldwide standard, but there are still dozens of different phone jacks in use worldwide. When local phone systems in countries around the world were designed, no one anticipated that people would one day bring their own communications devices from other countries and try to plug them into the local system. To do this, it's a good idea to make sure you have what you need before you leave.

Other issues to consider are whether the lines in modern hotels and offices are analog or digital. Digital lines carry an electrical current and can damage your equipment, but safety devices are available, such as the *IBM Modem Saver*, which detects whether a line is digital or analog, and the *TeleAdapt TeleSwitch Plus*, which allows you to safely connect to a digital phone line through the handset. Some digital phones have a separate jack, labeled *data port*, which is safe for modem connections.

There are also times when you may need to ignore the local dial tone, manually dial numbers to get online, switch between tone dialing and pulse dialing, or slow your modem down and change other settings through the modem's initialization string. For more information about how to make these changes in Windows 98 and Mac OS 8.5, see the *International Calls* section later in this chapter.

Another way to get around the difficulty in using a foreign dial tone and phone system may be to use the *AT&T Direct* service (www.att.com/traveler; 1-800-331-1140). AT&T Direct connects you to a U.S. dial tone through a local toll-free number and lets you place your calls this way. You may then have to go through a human operator and dial manually , but you can avoid this by downloading AT&T's free *Laptop Access Software* (www.att.com/business_traveler). Other long-distance phone companies offer similar services, as well.

Significant international charges still apply if you call the United States, even if you are dialing through a toll-free local number, but at times this may be the only way for you to connect. You might also need this kind of access if you are sending a fax through your modem or trying to connect remotely to a LAN.

Where to Find What You Need

Exact details about the phone and electrical requirements for every country around the world are too involved to go into here, but you can get more information—and any equipment you may need to make everything work—from a variety of sources.

Electronics stores such as *Radio Shack* (which also does business in North America, the United Kingdom, and Australia) carry adapters for the most commonly visited countries, but for more complete information and online ordering, try *Laptop Travel* (www.laptoptravel.com) or *TeleAdapt* (www.teleadapt.com). Both can provide information about exactly what is needed in each country around the world. They sell power- and phone-adapter kits for individual countries, regional packs for regions that use the same standard, and—for the truly nomadic—even kits with every possible power or phone adapter. Another source of information for travelers with computers is *Road-news.com* (www.roadnews.com).

TeleAdapt's offerings may be of particular interest because any purchaser of TeleAdapt products can get 24-hour technical support from TeleAdapt's offices in the United States (+1-877-835-3232 or +1-408 965 1400), Britain (+44-0-181-233-3000), and Australia (+61-0-2-9433-8363).

Keeping in mind the adapters you may need to use it, it can also be helpful to take along an extra length of phone cord to any country. This can help you connect your modem to phone jacks that are placed under a hotel bed or in another inconvenient location.

Internet Access for Travelers

With your equipment ready, you'll need to have access to the Internet or your online service. While you could, of course, dial back to a number that you use in your home country, international phone charges may add up quickly and make this prohibitively expensive. Remember that unlimited Net access through your Internet service provider doesn't exempt you from long-distance phone charges. If it's possible to arrange, a local option is better.

Local Internet Service Providers

If you're going to be staying in another country for an extended period of time—or at least long enough to justify the hassle and setup fees—it may make sense to simply sign up with a local Internet service provider. And if you don't happen to know your ISP options for Kuwait or Argentina, check *The List* (www.thelist.com), which provides one of the most comprehensive lists of ISPs by country. The

List has a profile of each listed ISP, along with details such as area codes served, platforms supported, support hours, dial-up services offered (you might be surprised by some of the countries where you can connect 56k, ISDN, or cable modems), as well as information on fees and taxes.

For more advanced Internet access (T1 access and so forth) in countries around the world, check the *Ascend Network Service Provider Directory* at http://isp.ascend.com.

International Options

If you're not staying in any one place long enough to justify signing up for a local Internet service provider, or if you are traveling through many different countries, it makes sense to use a service that operates internationally and has local dial-in numbers in a variety of cities. A lot of companies call this *Internet roaming,* and they call their local numbers *POPs,* for points of presence (not to be confused with post office protocol, also abbreviated POP, which is a standard for email).

At this point there are few truly global options with local access numbers in nearly every country. Most Internet service providers focus on one or a few countries, but notable exceptions include *iPass, GRIC Communications, EUNet,* and *IBM Internet Connection Services* (see the list that follows for details).

Most of the rest offer local numbers in at least several countries, usually in Western Europe, North America, Australia, Japan, and perhaps a few other countries as well, sometimes with additional surcharges. All of the options in the following list have local numbers in at least several countries.

America Online (AOL). Provides local dial-up numbers in several countries: Australia, Canada, Germany, France, the United Kingdom, Sweden, Japan, and Hong Kong. For more information, see www.aol.com/info/international.html.

AOL also has options for access from a much greater number of countries around the world through its *AOLGlobalNet* service. Surcharges between $6 and $24 per hour (at the time of writing) apply in addition to regular AOL fees. For more information about AOLGlobalNet, see http://intlaccess.web.aol.com, or use the AOL keyword *access* and press the International Access button.

AT&T WorldNet. Despite its name, AT&T WorldNet provides local access numbers only in the United States, Puerto Rico, the Virgin Islands, and Japan. For details, see www.att.com/worldnet.

CompuServe. CompuServe has extensive worldwide service. To find out about the countries you are interested in, go to CompuServe's access number finder on the Web at www.compuserve.com/content/phone/phone.asp.

Earthlink. Earthlink offers local numbers in Australia, Belgium, Canada, France, Germany, Hong Kong, Italy, Japan, Luxembourg, the Netherlands, Sweden, Switzerland, the United Kingdom, and the United States. For more details, see www.earthlink.net/home/access/numbers.html.

EUnet Traveller. One of the most truly global Internet service providers, EUnet Traveller provides local access numbers in Europe, the United States, Africa, Asia, and Australia. For more information, check the EUnet Traveller site at http://traveller.eu.net.

GRIC Communications. GRIC (www.gric.com) offers local dial-in numbers through a network of providers in 75 countries.

IBM Internet Connection Services. Not especially well known in the United States, IBM Internet Connection Services (http://ibm.net) offers access plans with local numbers in more than 50 countries, at prices comparable to those of more popular providers.

iPass True Global Internet Roaming. Providers for iPass (www.ipass.com) offer more than 3,000 local dial-in numbers in 150 countries. iPass doesn't offer Internet access directly to consumers, but makes arrangements with local ISPs to make their access numbers iPass-ready.

MCI Worldcom Internet. MCI's Internet service had local access numbers only in the United States as of early 1999. For more information, see www.mci.com.

Microsoft Network. Access to the Microsoft Network is available locally in the United States, Britain, and Japan. For more information, see http://free.msn.com/msncom/numbers/default.htm. MSN has also announced local language versions of its free Web-based email service Hotmail for French, German, and Japanese. For more information, see www.hotmail.com.

PSINet. PSINet (www.psinet.com) offers local access in North America, Western Europe, and Japan.

International Calls

For times when you haven't yet set up (or can't find) a local access number, it may be inevitable that you'll have to make an international call to an access number in another country. There are a couple of ways to minimize what can quickly add up to be a considerable expense, especially if you're doing any Web browsing and need to stay connected for more than just a couple of minutes to send and receive mail.

One way is to bill the charges to a calling card. Check with the company that issued your calling card first, but most can probably give you a rate that is lower (sometimes dollars a minute lower) than what you'll get if you simply place a call and let your hotel bill you.

Setting up your modem to handle calling cards is relatively simple with both Windows 98 and the Mac OS, and both allow you to set up configurations for different cities and to easily switch from one to the next.

In Windows, go to the Modem control panel, and open the *Dialing Properties* window, shown in Figure 4.1. This allows you to set preferences for different locations, such as local area, country, or city codes; prefixes for getting an outside line; and whether to use tone or pulse dialing. You can also select your long-distance carrier and enter your calling card information so that it will be ready when you connect.

Similar options are available in Mac OS 8.5 through the Remote Access control panel, shown in Figure 4.2. Under the RemoteAccess menu, select *DialAssist* to select from an (editable) list of countries, and to set dialing prefixes and preferences for a calling card. The RemoteAccess menu also provides a manual dialing option if your software doesn't produce the correct tones for your call to be put through the local phone system of another country.

Another helpful feature for users of Mac OS 8.5 is the *Location Manager* control panel, shown in Figure 4.3, which allows you to automatically switch the time zone of the computer's clock and other settings, including Remote Access modem settings, all at once by simply switching to a predefined location.

A somewhat similar control is offered in Windows by the *Regional Settings* control panel, shown in Figure 4.4, but this panel does not offer control over international dialing.

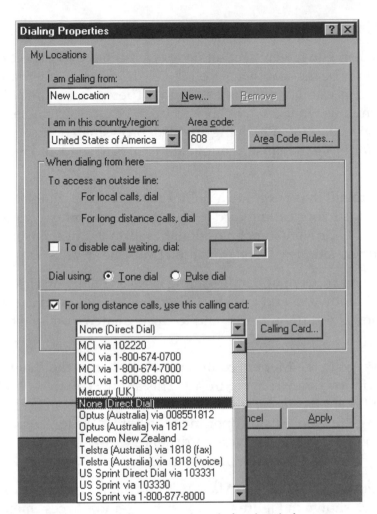

Figure 4.1 The Dialing Properties window in Windows 98.

Other Ways of Staying Connected Internationally

You don't necessarily need to have your own dial-up account to connect to your email while traveling abroad. If you have access to the Internet, you can, of course, get access to some email accounts through Telnet. You can also get more user-friendly access to post office protocol (POP)-based email accounts through services such as *MailStart* (www.mailstart.com), which allows you to check POP3 email accounts through a Web interface. Enter your email address and password, and

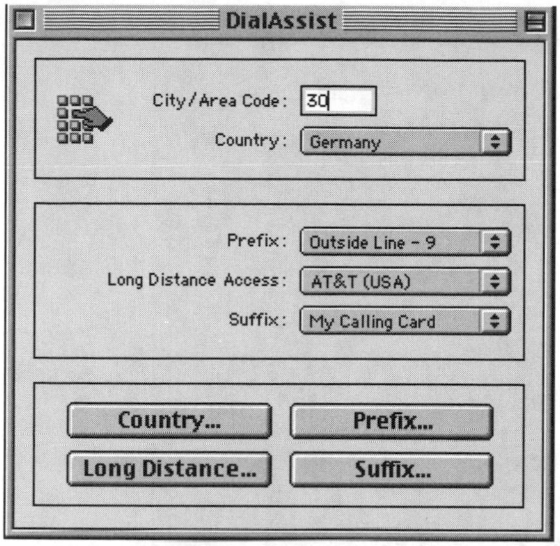

Figure 4.2 DialAssist in Mac OS 8.5.

MailStart will check your mail server and display any messages that you've received in the window of the Web browser you are using. The MailStart interface is also available in French, Spanish, and Portuguese. And if you're concerned that MailStart asks you to send your password through an unsecure connection, don't worry any more than you would with your regular email access. It's a requirement of the

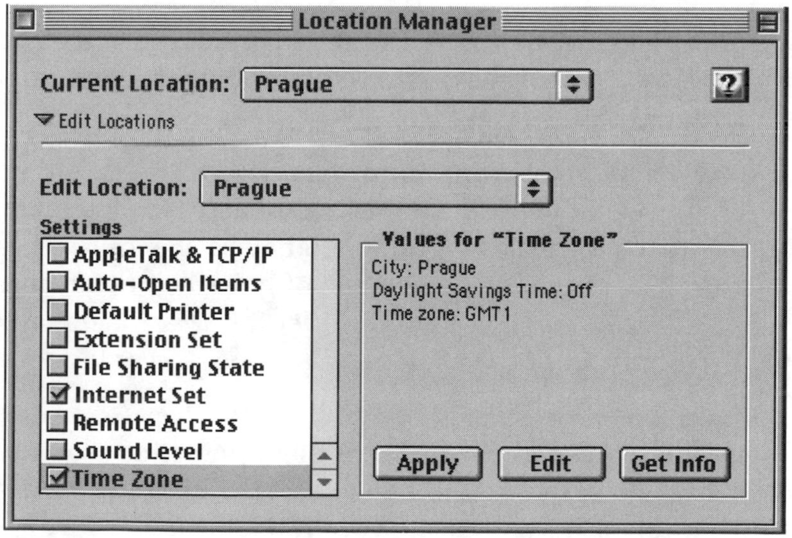

Figure 4.3 Location Manager in Mac OS 8.5.

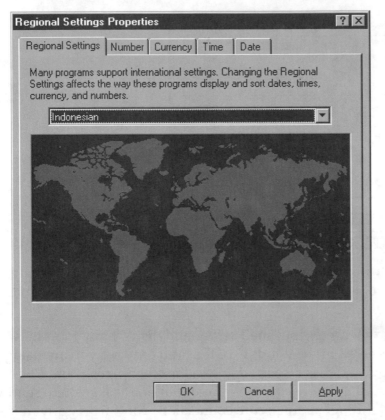

Figure 4.4 Regional Settings in Windows 98.

POP3 protocol that passwords be sent unencrypted, so you're doing it all the time this way anyway with the email client you ordinarily use. It's just more noticeable this way.

Checking your mail in this way—or using another Web-based mail system—assumes that you have some kind of access to the Internet already. This method can be helpful if you have a chance to use someone else's machine but don't want to reconfigure their email client to check your mail. Another option to consider for occasional mail checks is the growing number of cybercafés and Internet access kiosks around the world.

This may not be an ideal solution, but if there's no other way to get access in a city you're in—or you don't want to deal with the hassle of setting up a local ISP, reconfiguring your modem, and so forth—using cybercafés may make sense (besides, you may need a break and a chance to meet some people anyway). By early 1999, there were more than 2,500 cybercafés in more than 120 countries, plus more than 2,000 registered public Internet access points and kiosks.

For more information about cybercafés in the areas you will be traveling to, check the *Cybercafé Search Engine* at www.cybercaptive.com. You may be surprised by the number of cities that have them.

Language Learning Software

It may be that you don't simply need to work in another language— you might also need to learn it, or to brush up on language skills that you acquired years ago in school or as a child.

Your first idea might be to use a language CD-ROM product, but choosing one can be tricky. Many of the products available today are limited in what they can do (be especially wary of promises that you'll be "speaking like a native" in suspiciously short periods of time, like 30, 60, or 90 days), and they offer little or no improvement over the independent-study language courses that have already been available for years on records, tapes, and now audio CDs.

A notable exception to this is *Who is Oscar Lake?* from Language Publications Interactive (www.languagepub.com), which is available for Windows and Macintosh in Spanish, French, English, German, and Italian.

Interactivity in Who is Oscar Lake? is sort of like the interactive world of a game like Myst, only in another language. Don't expect to sit down and have a chat with Oscar Lake, but the CD-ROM does allow you to hear and use language in about as realistic a way as is currently possible with computers. The program sends you on a mission to recover a stolen diamond, and your detective work takes you through a well done, slightly eerie multimedia world of train stations, hotel rooms, restaurants, and museums. It gives you a limited ability to interact with a variety of characters, some of whom are helpful, and some of whom are out to get you.

Programs like this can help you to use a language, but there are still inevitable limits. Language is ultimately about communication, and even working with the most interactive computer program can't be the beginning and end of language instruction for one simple reason:

Computers don't yet communicate or experience the world in a remotely human way.

Until they do (and if they ever do), computer language instruction materials are not likely to be more than helpful supplements. As convenient as it would be for each of us to have an infinitely patient language tutor for $49.95, it may always be necessary to practice in live, spontaneous situations with real human beings to truly learn a spoken language. Let the buyer beware.

Portable Electronic Translators

Portable electronic translators—both personal digital assistants with language software, such as the PalmPilot, and specialized devices created especially for this purpose—can be helpful (or simply fun), but they should be chosen with care. Devices and applications that are technically sound may be based on poor language-to-language dictionaries.

A good test before you buy is to look up words in your own language that have more than one meaning, and see if the translations you are presented with are explained. If you translate the English word *glasses*, for example, does your translator tell you which translation means drinking glasses and which is for eyeglasses? If it doesn't, who knows what kind of trouble you could get yourself into.

These kinds of detailed explanations are the hallmarks of good print dictionaries. Expect at least this much in electronic dictionaries and translators, as well.

Next

The four chapters of Part One have covered all the things you need to know to support work in multiple languages on your own computer, as well as options for getting support and staying connected while traveling. Part Two discusses the development of multilingual applications, and the creation of customized language resources that aren't available from other sources.

Developing Multilingual Applications and International Solutions

CHAPTER 5

Strategies for Multilingual Development and Internationalization

E ven if your organization doesn't already have to deal with multilingual computing issues, now may be a good time to start thinking about them. If there is any possibility that you will be expanding internationally in the future, then laying the right foundations for multilingual support—in your IT resources, your Internet presence, the applications you develop, or simply in your own work—can help you avert serious problems in the future. In the long run, it is much easier to put in the extra effort at the beginning to plan appropriately for multilingual support than to sort through a snarl of language-encoding conflicts, incompatibilities, and work that needs to be redone in order to be truly ready for the rest of the world. This chapter discusses how to make choices and plans that will help carry you and your organization into a more multilingual future.

Of course, one chapter cannot go into every detail of what is necessary to plan, implement, and manage multilingual strategies and support for a global project or organization, and, in fact, entire consulting businesses are built around providing this know-how. But if you are an IT professional who needs to keep in step with—or be responsible for—the internationalization of your organization and its products or services, this chapter will give you a better idea of the most important issues to keep in mind.

Thinking Internationally throughout an Organization

The internationalization of an organization and its products and services can be an enormous undertaking. Unless your organization is very small, successful internationalization will require a great deal of cooperation. Even if you are currently in business by yourself, the more groundwork you lay for multilingual expansion, the better your position will be when things start to take off.

A product or service that is (or eventually will be) meant for a global, multilingual market requires broad support in order to succeed. Those who develop, market, sell, or play other roles in creating and offering your products and services will all need to keep multilingual requirements (and payoffs, which are discussed later in this chapter) in mind. Not only that, but all this support and cooperation has to be well coordinated. Having a new application localized won't do much good if localized versions of the documentation aren't ready, or if a culturally appropriate marketing plan hasn't been developed, or if your tech-support people aren't ready to field questions in other languages, and so on.

Remember that taking the steps to make sure that all these things are in place won't simply be a matter of translating or adapting what you already have and the way you already do things for use in another language or location. For example, promotional materials or packages may not only need to be translated, they may need to be completely redesigned to make the best possible impression in another culture. The ways in which you explain, market, sell, and support an application or service in different parts of the world may need to be rethought from the ground up.

While it may be necessary to do this rethinking for each individual market, it is also important to think of internationalization as a whole, rather than taking a piecemeal approach to succeeding internationally in several local markets. Later discussion in this chapter shows that keeping the international big picture in mind can help all your individual local efforts.

Understanding Internationalization

At the outset, it's important to clear up a few things.

You might find the terms *internationalization* and *localization* used together even though they might seem at first to be exact opposites. What could be less international than something local?

One way to keep these terms straight is to think of localization as just a part of the process of internationalization. The whole international world is made up of lots of different individual places or locales. *Internationalization* means laying the groundwork for a product to work properly in any or all of these locales by making sure that locale-specific features (such as language) are not hard-coded into the product. *Localization* means translating and customizing a properly internationalized product for one or more specific locales. The result is that with minimal changes to an application's source code, it can be adapted for locales around the world.

NOTE
This chapter discusses some general internationalization design issues, while coding issues are discussed in greater detail in Chapter 6, "Developing Multilingual Applications." Localization is discussed in Chapter 8, "Translation and Localization."

It is important to remember that localization is not simply a matter of language, however. The real issue is not about language but locale.

For computing purposes, *locale* is defined as the set of preferences or conventions that is associated with the user's location, in addition to the user's language. A simple example of the difference between a language and a locale is the difference between U.S. English and British English. Differences that software must take into account include not only differences in spelling (a language issue) but also differences in currency, and in date formats.

"After a product completes the lengthy development cycle, it can easily be shot down in the marketplace by something as simple as one wrong term or a misplaced flag or inaccurate map," says Tom Edwards, a geographer who heads Microsoft's Geopolitical Product Strategy group. "Even one, seemingly minor mistake can prevent a product from being distributed in the intended locale."

The characteristics of a locale can also include things like sort order, input methods, and formats for time, numbers, names, addresses, and phone numbers. Christopher Hanaoka, director of worldwide research and development for Bowne Global Solutions, says that it's surprisingly common for inserts and special promotional materials for a localized product to make it to the final stages before someone says, "Hey, people in Europe can't use an 800 number!" Cultural factors can come into play, as well. For example, educational products geared for children may need to take into account different expectations.

"In Japan, the way they teach multiplication is through rhymes," Hanaoka says. If you're thinking of localizing an educational product that doesn't use this approach, it's important to be aware of the obstacles you may face.

Another more business-oriented cultural assumption was built into software designed to help allocate product placement "face space" in a supermarket. The product made assumptions about supermarket layout that were based on typical U.S. supermarkets. It was ill-suited to the global marketplace because supermarkets in other countries may work differently. For example, they may require payment at individual counters in the store for certain items instead of having a single checkout area before the exit.

I18N? L10N?

Reading about globalization issues, you might come across the terms *I18N* or *L10N*. These aren't standards, organizations, or protocols, they're simply abbreviations in which the digits stand for the number of letters that have been left out. I18N is a common abbreviation for *internationalization* and means "I-18 letters-N." L10N is a common abbreviation for *localization* and stands for "L-10 letters-N."

Clarifying the Need for Internationalization

In addition to the need to understand the difference between language and locale, it is important to clearly identify the importance of internationalizing your products and efforts, and to make sure that everyone in your organization understands what is at stake. What new markets could be opened up? What are the sales projections for localized versions of your products? Could your organization's image and brand get a boost from a product that is successful globally, not just in one country?

Hanaoka suggests asking a few key questions before beginning a globalization effort or seeking the help of an outside vendor to help with the globalization of a product. The following questions will help to identify requirements and create reasonable budgets:

- What kind of sales do you expect in the target locales? What kind of market research has been performed to validate these estimates?

- What kind of support (such as technical support hot lines, staff, and so forth) do you plan to have in the target locales? Are there any conflicts with distributors who may want (or not want) this responsibility?

- What kind of marketing campaign do you plan to have in the target locales? If your product was developed initially for the U.S. market, does it have special promotional materials (such as inserts with phone numbers, addresses, and so forth) that are valid only for the United States?

- What kind of locale-specific content do you envision for the target locale? Will your distributor (if there is one) want to have involvement in choosing this locale-specific content?

- What kind of reviews are required due to distribution agreements? It is often the case that, after the fact, a local distributor decides to provide additional subjective input to a finalized product, requiring the final delivered product to undergo another phase of changes.

- Has the source code undergone any internationalization? Does the code need to be tested to ensure internationalization? Is this something that you have the internal bandwidth and expertise to perform, or do you plan to outsource?

Answering or, at least, considering these questions at the outset is important. "Unfortunately," Hanaoka cautions, "the lack of proper insight into globalization often results in schedule delays, unexpected costs, or poor market acceptance."

Clarifying the need to think internationally about products and services also has a positive side. It can turn what otherwise might be seen as a huge and burdensome logistical undertaking into an important part of what your organization does. If this understanding spares you from having to do the work required for internationalization as an awkward, time-consuming afterthought, it can also mean significant savings in money, effort, and energy.

Microsoft's Geopolitical Product Strategy Group

The cultural issues that affect product globalization are complex—so complex that Microsoft has established a group intended exclusively to examine the issue.

"When I created Geopolitical Product Strategy," says Tom Edwards, a geographer who heads the GPS group, "the intention was to create a centralized body within Microsoft to act as a node of information for critical and sensitive content, as far as how it affects Microsoft markets and the ability to maintain product sales." Edwards says that Microsoft's GPS group is the most ambitious effort made by a private company to identify potential localization problems.

Unfortunately for the rest of us, Edwards says most of this information won't be made public. He said competitors have used locale-sensitive issues to undermine Microsoft products in some markets. However, the results of his group's research can be seen in Microsoft products such as the Encarta Interactive World Atlas, the Encarta Encyclopedia, Bookshelf, and many others from games to office software.

One thing to keep in mind is that there are no easy answers—no single source to turn to for advice about issues that may potentially affect the success of a localization product. This is especially true for a new product that may not have been tried in a particular locale before.

"The real key is reading and researching as many sources as possible, from as many locales as possible. Diversity in your information is key," Edwards says. "You cannot swallow the first bit of information that comes along and appears to confirm your hunch. You must take it all in and weigh source reliability, dates, and many other factors to arrive at a decision that is right for your purpose. Also, it's very important not to just absorb book information. Getting in touch with people in the various locales and coming to know their viewpoints firsthand is critical."

Edwards also warns that problematic cultural assumptions can crop up anywhere. "Editors may miss certain terms or phrases, developers may miss something in a string of code, designers might employ the wrong symbol, cartographers may use the wrong place name on a map, and so forth. We approach the issues generally from a content viewpoint: by the kinds of content that may appear in a software product. These can include terminology, text strings, code strings and abbreviations, maps (there are many issues with these), clip art of flags and symbols, sounds, address formats, and so forth. In short, anything that has to do with geography and culture is suspect.

"This makes for a very broad field of content that must be considered by GPS. Being a small team, we cannot possibly catch every possible problem, and therefore we work hard to make Microsoft groups aware of where problems could exist. Then it is the responsibility of those individual groups—working with GPS—to catch the errors and correct them before the product ships."

A good example of one potentially contentious issue that is often overlooked between locales is found in lists of countries. "Country lists are used in menus for various purposes, and oftentimes different product groups construct their list from various sources. GPS maintains an official list for Microsoft, but groups are still not fully aware of this fact. So we often get lists with incorrect names, sensitive names, and non-countries (like Kurdistan) in the list. It's important for Microsoft or any company to be consistent with this type of information."

Another example is found in central Asia and affects products—potentially everything from reference works to business software to clip art—distributed in India, Pakistan, and China.

"The region of Jammu and Kashmir in central Asia is very contentious and continues to be a potential geopolitical flash point. The problem this presents for software is that the respective governments who claim this area all have strict demands for how maps must appear. In India, for example, the official policy is that all of Jammu and Kashmir is Indian. Therefore, all maps produced in India or imported into India must show this region as Indian—not as disputed or claimed or anything but Indian territory. Many companies, including Microsoft, have made the mistake of not heeding this policy, and have subsequently had their products recalled or banned." Another similar issue is found in mainland China, where the government forbids any use of the term Republic of China in reference to Taiwan, as well as the Taiwanese flag, calendar, and so forth.

These are complex issues that may be hard to foresee at the outset, and it may be helpful to make people throughout your organization aware of the need to look at the localization of products from as many angles as possible.

There currently are no comprehensive guides to political and cultural issues that can affect internationally distributed software, but Edwards suggests the following sources as starting points for research:

- *Reordering the World: Geopolitical Perspectives on the Twenty-First Century*, edited by George Demko and William Wood (Westview Press, 1999).

- *Standing Your Ground: Territorial Disputes and International Conflict,* by Paul Kuth (University of Michigan Press, 1998).

- *The Statesman's Year-Book: The Essential Political and Economic Guide to All the Countries of the World,* edited by Barry Turner (St. Martin's Press,1998).

- *The CIA World Factbook,* www.odci.gov/cia/publications/factbook/index.html.

Be Clear about Who Is Responsible

Clarifying the need for internationalization and research into the complex issues involved isn't enough. Making sure that everyone in your organization whose work could potentially have an impact on internationalization is aware of its importance is necessary, but this doesn't mean that it can be a grassroots effort. You may need formal accountability.

Because of the complexity involved in internationalization and the costly and time-consuming consequences when mistakes are made and need to be corrected in several localized versions, it is important to make it clear where authority and accountability lies. There needs to be extensive communication and cooperation for internationalization to be a success, but key players need to be responsible for ensuring that it happens.

Depending on your organization, it may also make sense for someone to have an exclusive responsibility for internationalization. Adding it on to someone's existing responsibilities may simply mean that it tends to fall by the wayside and is not given the priority it deserves.

The Details of Internationalization

If one or more of the aspects of your global effort fails or is out of step with the rest, it can seriously bog down the development, release, or sales of a product or service in the global market.

This can happen in any project in which one person's work depends on another's, but it is a particular concern with internationalization because there is a kind of multiplier effect. If something isn't done right, it doesn't just have to be corrected, it may have to be corrected in every localized version of your product, plus its documentation, and in other related materials. A single mistake can require dozens of time-consuming corrections.

How can you avoid this? What do you need to keep in mind at each step of the way to make sure that this doesn't happen?

Information about choosing multilingual operating systems, applications, and fonts is provided in Chapter 1, "The World-Ready Computer," and Chapter 2, "World-Savvy Applications." Planning for multilingual support, however, isn't just a matter of choosing the right resources to run on your organization's desktop computers and laptops. The danger in this approach is that different segments of an organization—a few individuals who use different languages, or whole departments—may all find solutions that suit them individually, but the sum of these individual solutions will not be a unified approach to language support.

The following issues take a broader look at internationalization. They are discussed in greater detail throughout the rest of the book, but the following sections provide an overview of what needs to be kept in mind and why.

Compatibility: Unicode

As discussed in Chapter 3, "Multilingual Compatibility Issues," one of the most important issues to be aware of when planning for multilingual work is the arrival of the international character set Unicode. With few exceptions, new projects that will require multilingual support should be based in Unicode and conform to its consistent standard for representing the world's hundreds of languages in computer code. Most industry heavy-hitters, including Microsoft, are now committed to Unicode and are making their products Unicode-compliant.

Fortunately, much of the work in implementing Unicode has been done for you. Applications ranging from common productivity applications to enterprise-level servers are beginning to offer Unicode support, and programming tools that make it easier for developers to implement Unicode are available, as well.

NOTE

The Multilingual Information Society (www2.echo.lu/mlis/en/home.html) provides news and information about the language industry and language markets in the European Union, as well as a venue for promoting new multilingual applications that support European languages.

Globalized Code-Base

Another factor to look for in applications and operating systems that you depend on is multilingual support through a single code-base. In the past, different localized versions of applications and operating systems essentially meant that there could be dozens of slightly different versions in simultaneous use throughout the same organization. These could be cumbersome to deploy and support, especially for tech-support personnel who were unfamiliar with all of the languages in different user interfaces.

A more sophisticated way of providing multilingual support is for applications and the operating systems they run under to use the same code-base regardless of language, and to make it possible for support for one or more additional languages to be turned on or off as needed.

Microsoft is one company that is embracing this single-code-base strategy, both at the OS level in Windows 2000 and in applications such as Office 2000.

Windows 2000, for example, will support more than 100 language locales (examples of different locales for the same language would be the People's Republic of China and Taiwan for Chinese, or France and Canada for French), and this support will ship with every version. According to F. Avery Bishop, program manager of Microsoft's multilingual developer communications, a "dairy farmer in Vermont will be able to install the files required to input and display Chinese, Arabic, Hindi, Thai, Vietnamese, etc. They all come on the standard U.S. English Windows 2000 CD, and every other version of Windows 2000."

There will still, however, be localized versions of the user interface, as well as a Windows 2000 Multilanguage Version (www.microsoft.com/ globaldev/faqs/multilang.asp), available for Windows 2000 Server and Windows 2000 Professional (the planned successor to Windows 98). Although not currently planned as a retail product, the multilanguage version will allow large corporations to roll out Windows 2000 for users of different languages with a single installer, allowing users to change the user interface to one of about two dozen languages as a preference.

The main difference between Windows 2000 Multilanguage Version and individual localized versions is that not all items, such as folders and file names, will be localized. Instead, they will remain in the master language of the system, making it easier to support. Tech-support personnel unfamiliar with the languages of individual users will also be able to temporarily set the interface to their own language to find and fix problems.

Other companies, such as Apple, are taking their products in this direction, as well. Peter Lowe, Apple's Mac OS product line manager, says, "Our plan for the future is to continue to integrate multilingual capabilities into the mainstream product so that users don't have to buy any additional components. We want to have one code-base worldwide," The difference between different language versions would be "mainly just the scripts and fonts that are added to it to make it appropriate."

Apple hasn't yet decided when the transition to full multilingual support in the mainstream operating system will be complete, but given the fact that Mac OS 8.5 has already shipped significant portions of the support included in six of Apple's seven language kits, completion of the transition can't be far off. Lowe says that two of the most important considerations affecting what to include are how easy it is to use the code, and whether support for the languages could be included without adding royalty fees to every copy of the Mac OS. "The byproduct of that kind of architecture has been that we're able to support multilingual computing on a single platform," Lowe says. "We've tried to make the operating system as generic as possible with regard to language."

Apple plans to take that integration of multilingual capabilities down to the application level, as well. Not only would a user be able to work with multiple languages on a single system, as is possible now, but Apple would like users to be able to have the system or the application change languages as needed. Menus, commands, input methods, standards for handling numbers, dates, and times, for example, could be set for one language or another as simply as changing a preference, thus eliminating the need to localize the operating system and applications into dozens of languages. One user could use an individual machine entirely in Japanese, and minutes later, another user could be using it in Hebrew.

Apple has not specified when these options will debut in the Mac OS, but the technology Apple acquired when it bought Next's OpenStep supports the ability to completely abstract user interface from the code. "The technology that has made that possible is something that we're going to be looking at for Mac OS X," says Lowe. Mac OS X (10) is the next major release of the Mac OS, planned for release in late 1999.

Regardless of which operating system you use, using applications and operating systems with a single code-base regardless of language can make language support significantly easier and less expensive. Some software companies are leading the way to make this single-code-base strategy for language support standard in their products, but others aren't there yet. When choosing software to buy and use in a multilingual environment, applications and operating systems that use a single code-base regardless of language may deserve special consideration.

Development and Design

Whenever possible, developers should lay multilingual foundations in the applications they create, even for languages that aren't yet supported. This may seem obvious, especially given the amount of time and trouble it can save when it comes time to localize, but still not everyone does it. "There are still people coding without the benefit of the last 15 years of localization experience," observes Ben Sargent, the Web content director for Bowne Global Solutions, a globalization-services company.

Developing applications that are independent of locale and thereby easily localizable is a broad subject. It is discussed in greater detail in Chapter 6, but one simple illustration is that in Windows code, you can use setlocale to specify a locale instead of coding outputs in a single format that will not be appropriate in every locale. Developers should also use file formats that are easier to localize, such as resource files instead of hard-coded strings for any text that may need to be translated.

Christopher Hanaoka, Bowne's director of worldwide research and development, also cautions that the Web has opened up new places for old internationalization problems to crop up. "For Windows applications you have resource files where all the strings reside," he notes, which makes string localization easier. "That same kind of thing can't be applied to the Web."

New developers who are most experienced in coding for the Web may be unaware of internationalization issues that other developers with more experience developing for platforms such as Windows may already be aware of.

"There's a lot more developers now than there were before, and I see a lot of the problems that we stopped seeing a few years ago starting to emerge with JavaScript, VisualBasic script, and things like that," Hanaoka says.

Yet another issue to bear in mind is the design of an application's user interface. An icon that in the United States represents a personal mailbox, for example, may look like some kind of tunnel in other parts of the world where mail is delivered through door slots or in other ways. Similarly, space should be left for menu names and dialog boxes that may be longer in translation than they are in the original language. To make localization as easy as possible, all elements of an application should be as locale- and language-independent as possible.

Overall, it makes sense to move to procedures in which the development of your English product (or whatever your primary-language version is) includes all of these localization considerations.

Documentation

Documentation should ideally be written in language that is relatively easy to translate, and it should avoid locale-specific cultural references (for instance, the Superbowl, the 4th of July, and so forth). It should also be laid out in a way (using extra white space, for example) that allows for expansion or contraction if the translated version turns out to be longer (or shorter, although this is less common if you are starting from English) than the original version. You may also want to aim for simpler graphics that use less text since graphics files are generally more difficult to localize than plain text.

See Chapter 8, "Translation and Localization," for more advice about developing documentation for an international application, and details about writing for easier translatability.

Localization and Translation

Sufficient time needs to be allowed for the localization of a product and all collateral materials, such as documentation. Documentation alone may involve the translation of thousands of pages, depending on how long your documentation is and how many languages it needs to be translated into. See Chapter 8 for a more in-depth look at these issues.

Another localization factor to keep in mind is the importance of simultaneous localization. It can be important that localized versions of applications not lag too far behind the release of the primary language version.

For example, if it takes a year to localize your product, you may already be close to the next major release of the primary-language version. Potential buyers may simply decide to wait for the localized version of that release, not the one you have just painstakingly localized. Localization that is fast, or, better yet, simultaneous, can be key to the success of a localized product. "Time really is money when it comes to localized products. It's very important to have simultaneous release," says Hanaoka. "The shelf life of a product is so short that if you have an extra two months on the shelf, obviously, that can mean a lot of money." Fortunately, Hanaoka says, simultaneous localization shouldn't be too difficult to achieve if there's a partnership with localization.

See Chapter 8 for more advice about working with a localization service provider (or for coordinating your in-house localization efforts).

Marketing

Marketing materials have to be developed specifically for the target language and community they are meant for, not merely translated, for the best chances of success. You may need to reconsider slogans that cannot be easily translated to other languages. Certain types of lettering may need to be avoided because text in some colors can have unwanted associations, including death, religion, royalty, pornography, treason, and the intent to kill. You may even need to reconsider your product's name. The story about the Chevy Nova, alleged to have sold poorly in Mexico because *no va* means "it doesn't go" in Spanish, is actually just a legend (the car sold well), but you would do well to check your product's name for obviously embarrassing overlaps in the native language.

Unfortunately, there can be no easy checklist of such things to avoid, but Chapter 8, has more information about what you can do to localize marketing efforts.

Legal

Your legal experts may need to look into international copyright issues and regulations governing software exports. For starters, check the U.S. Copyright Office's statement on international copyright (http://lcweb.loc.gov/copyright/fls/fl100) and the Law Forum (www.lawforum.net/firms/copyrights.htm) for listings of firms that deal with international copyright issues.

Some European governments have also enacted laws that require products imported into their countries to be accompanied by full documentation in their official languages. For details about regulations in the European Union, see the E.U. External Information Office's page at http://europa.eu.int/en/comm/dg10/infcom/external.html, and for details on export rules, see the American Alliance for Software Exports (www.aase.org) and the Software Publishers Association Global pages (www.spa.org/intl).

NOTE

An in-depth article about the preparation and resources that are required to successfully export software is available from *Bottom Up,* an online magazine for high-tech ventures, at www.bottom-up.com/marketing/mk-981201.shtml.

Sales and Distribution

Your sales and distribution departments need to be ready for international inquiries and able to accept and distribute international orders, perhaps paid for in different currencies. If necessary, it is important to make sure your mail server can handle extended ASCII characters, or your back-end server can handle two-byte characters. Server issues are discussed in greater detail in Chapter 9, "Multilingual Electronic Communication."

Technical Support

Your technical-support staff must be familiar with the localized versions of your products and needs to be ready to handle the main languages in which help may be requested. You may need to be able to provide support throughout the night and early morning to accommodate users in different parts of the world, or open offices (or contract for support services) in the countries where your products are available.

It's also important to decide at the outset who will be responsible for support. Hanaoka says support misunderstandings are one of the most common problems he sees for localized products. "The U.S. people thought that the distributor was going to be supporting it and the distributor thought the U.S. people were going to be supporting it." Depending on your existing support infrastructure, making last-minute arrangements to support localized products can mean delays "anywhere from a couple days to a couple months, to the product never making it to the mass market," Hanaoka warns.

Sharing Information

Will everyone in your organization—or its clients and customers—be able to access and use any information resource they need, without having to worry about language encoding compatibility? This is another important question to bear in mind when globalizing an organization's computing resources.

It is important to note that this doesn't mean that instant, automatic translation of any textual data from one language to another should be available to everyone (although in some cases this is becoming possible). It should, however, be possible to access and use information in other languages, as appropriate, with a minimum of technical difficulty. For example, it should be possible for those with access privileges to use the same database without regard to language. It should be possible for your organization to keep different language versions of the same information up to date in a relatively straightforward manner and on a manageable schedule. If information has been provided in (or translated to) a particular language, that information should be easily accessible to the employees or customers who need it.

Updating Information

Vianna Quock is vice president of globalization services for Uniscape, Inc. (www.uniscape-inc.com), a multilingual solutions provider. Quock says that one of the most important things to keep in mind when globalizing a company's information resources is the amount of time that will be needed to do it. This is especially true if information is updated frequently.

"The problem is to ensure the information is consistent among all other languages," says Quock. If the same information is being made available in different language versions through a Web page, for example, it is necessary to consider how long it will take for all the languages in use to be translated, and to have strategies in place to make sure it happens as consistently and efficiently as possible. Maintaining this kind of consistency becomes even more important the more often that this information is updated.

Database Design

Your information resources may be multilingual, but what does this mean? Are they simply available in distinct language versions, or will individual documents use several languages? Will data in several languages be stored in the same database?

"Database design will be critical," Quock says. If you have an existing database that supports only one language, that single-language design "will need to be completely changed so that all rows with 'translatable' information will be duplicated with a language index. All select, update, and insert statements to access data will need to make use of the user language."

A Common Pitfall: Hacking a Solution

One of the dangers in adding multilingual support is doing it piecemeal. You might have a database application working in English, but then need to add Japanese support. You do this and everything is fine, but then you need to add support for other languages, too, and you may either end up redoing a lot of your original work, or running into conflicts and incompatibilities.

"The big mistake is usually to 'hack' a solution for one particular language," says Quock. "This can be relatively fast to implement. But it will create a nightmare when they decide to go with more languages. The key is to create one application for all languages, not one application for one language."

One example of a hacked solution that Quock suggests is found in the way that dates are handled. The U.S. date format is MM/DD/YYYY (in other words, 12/31/1999 for December 31, 1999). Developers who want to make their applications work for the Japanese market can simply change this to the Japanese date format, which is YYYY/MM/DD. This works fine until the application has to work in yet another locale, such as France, where the date format is typically DD/MM/YYYY, or Germany, where it is DD.MM.YYYY.

"All related source code has to be changed again," said Quock. "The correct solution is not to hard-code any format, but at application runtime to find out which country that user wants and format accordingly." Quock points out that similar problems can arise with formatting time, addresses, numbers, and currency, or when assumptions are made about which character sets will be used.

Don't Be Daunted by Complexity

Especially in the United States, most people are only well acquainted with one or two languages. The prospect of having to understand the basics of several languages, each with different writing systems and requirements, can be daunting. For large projects, it may be wise to seek the help of consultants and firms that specialize in internationalization and localization, but even then, the process can be intimidating. It doesn't have to be.

Kamal Mansour, manager of non-Latin products for Monotype, Inc. (www.monotype.com), says it's important to have a good basic idea at the outset of how the writing systems work for the languages you need to deal with. "But that's a lot to explore for most people," he says. "Most people come asking naive questions and the danger is that they walk away immediately when they find out what's involved."

As an example, Mansour stresses that building in support for Unicode—which provides a structure for dealing with much of this linguistic complexity—can be easier than it seems at first.

"A lot of people when approaching Unicode for the first time see its huge size," he says. "That's typically based on a misunderstanding that in order to handle Unicode you have to handle every possible character in Unicode. That's not quite the case."

Building in support for Unicode doesn't necessarily require including support for all of Unicode, but simply allowing for that possibility in the future. In other words, if you need an application to handle East Asian languages, there is no need to build in complete support for Arabic, as well.

"They need to put in the scaffolding for all of Unicode. They don't need to build all the parts of Unicode," says Mansour. "A lot of people think it's an all or nothing exercise, but that really is not the case."

Legacy Issues

Another aspect of a globalization effort that you may have to deal with is legacy data that for one reason or another was created in a nonstandard language encoding. This may not necessarily be anyone's fault—you may have begun keeping the data before the arrival of the Unicode standard, for instance—but it is still your problem to deal with.

It is important to remember that there are usually ways to convert this legacy data. "As long as you know what the old character set was, there's no reason to abandon it," says Mansour. "There's tremendous support for older character sets," he said.

"Systems are coming more and more with conversion software," Mansour says, such as Java's ByteToCharConverter and CharToByteConverter classes (see http://java.sun.com/products/jdk/1.1/intl/html/intlspec.doc7.html for more details). But even if you have to prepare a converter yourself (or pay someone to do it for you) converting from one known character set to another can usually be done as a batch process in which the code points for one character set are simply converted to the code points for the other.

For more details, see Chapter 7, "Creating and Converting Multilingual Resources."

Getting Outside Help

See the magazine *MultiLingual Computing & Technology* (www .multilingual.com) for listings of companies that can provide help with internationalization, or see the companion site for this book (www.wiley.com/compbooks/ott) for the Web sites of companies that have contributed advice and insight.

Planning Tools for Multilingual Project Management

The previous section discusses some of the broader issues that need to be kept in mind when approaching a multilingual project from a management standpoint. But when it comes to actually planning the details of a multilingual project and monitoring the progress of that project, it can be helpful to have tools that are up to the job.

Perhaps the best-known project-management software, *Microsoft Project*, is available in a variety of localized versions, such as French and Japanese. U.S. English versions can handle most languages that use the Latin alphabet with the proper support installed, but check World Language Resources (www.worldlanguage.com) for the availability of fully localized versions in the United States.

Another project-management tool with support for several Latin-alphabet languages is *Webster* for Primavera 2.1. Webster also enables members of a team to see their assignments across multiple projects through a Web browser. English, French, German, Spanish, Italian, and Brazilian Portuguese are supported.

A Free Cost-Benefit Estimator

Language Partners International makes available an application called *Cost-Benefit Estimator,* a spreadsheet-based tool that helps users keep translation projects within budget by estimating costs and the resulting benefits of using various translation database systems in the translation process. The Cost-Benefit Estimator makes a prediction of the number of months (or words translated) before the system pays for itself. Price schedules for popular translation tools such as TRADOS, Star Transit, and Déjà Vu are included, or users can create their own customized price schedules. The Cost-Benefit Estimator can be downloaded for free from www.languagepartners.com/downloads.cbe.

Another free tool is *Maxim,* from Foreign Exchange Translators (www.fxtrans .com), an Excel-based tool for buyers of multilingual services. Maxim allows buyers of multilingual services to enter project details and to see the financial impact of adding documents, languages, or different requirements. Users eventually have to contact vendors for actual price quotes, but Maxim also provides a framework for estimating and understanding these quotes. An online help system for Maxim also provides negotiating tips and calls attention to potential problems and opportunities for time savings.

For more information about the translation tools mentioned here, see Chapter 8.

Keeping on Top of Language Issues

Many computer periodicals—both those for typical users and for programmers and developers—carry occasional articles about multilingual issues. However, you still might get the impression that getting computers to work in languages other than English is not much of an issue. It is.

An excellent source of information about multilingual computing issues is the magazine *MultiLingual Computing & Technology*, published six times a year. The magazine carries new product announcements and reviews, a calendar of upcoming events worldwide, and expert articles about multilingual computing issues and new developments. There is also an extensive buyer's guide with information about multi-lingual products, services, and consultants, and the magazine has a Web site at www.multilingual.com with selections from each issue's content. A free email newsletter called *LanguageTech Net News* is also available from editor Seth Thomas Schneider, providing information about new products and developments. For more information, see the magazine's Web site, or call 1-208-263-8178.

Another source is *Le Journal: The Journal of Record for Human Language Technology* (www.linglink.lu/lejournal/index.asp). Published by the European Commission and available in English, French, Spanish, German, and Italian, *Le Journal* provides news, analysis, and interviews about language technology.

You may also be interested in *Language International: The Magazine for Language Professionals* (www.language-international.com). Although not exclusively technical in its focus, *Language International* has articles on language technology and language project management, along with reviews of books and listings of upcoming events.

Next

Having looked at the broader issues involved in multilingual development and internationalization, it is now possible to take a closer look at development requirements, details, and tools in the next chapter.

6

Developing Multilingual Applications

This chapter provides an overview of what needs to be kept in mind when developing multilingual applications, along with the multilingual aspects of major platforms, and the tools that are available to make multilingual development easier.

This chapter doesn't delve deeply into coding issues (entire books have been written on just the multilingual aspects of this subject), but it does provide a look at the major issues involved in multilingual development, along with sources for more detailed information.

Issues in Multilingual Application Development

Multilingual development is related to—but not identical to—the subject of software localization. *Localization* is the process of actually preparing applications for use in other locales around the world; this is discussed in more detail in Chapter 8, "Translation and Localization." Laying the groundwork for easier localization is important, but there is more to multilingual development.

It is possible to develop individual localized versions of an application that are essentially monolingual or bilingual. For example, a localized application might be optimized for only U.S. English, or it might deal best with a language pair, such as U.S. English and Japanese.

A multilingual application, on the other hand, can be used more widely, and is easier to adapt for specific locales than an application that supports only one or two writing systems. To be truly multilingual, an application should include the foundations for supporting many—or all—writing systems in the same version. The following sections detail the most important factors involved in developing multilingual applications.

Support for Unicode

Building in support for the global Unicode character set is one of the most important requirements for multilingual support—both today, as Unicode begins to become more widely accepted, and especially in the future, when it is likely to become the global equivalent of ASCII.

Enabling for Unicode with Backward Compatibility for Windows 9x

If you need to write Unicode-enabled applications for Windows 95, Windows 98, and Windows NT/2000, you run into a problem: Windows 9x has only limited support for Unicode. How can you get around this?

One option is to create two versions, one for Windows NT/2000 that uses Unicode and another for Windows 9x that uses the American National Standards Institute (ANSI) standard (essentially ASCII). This option, however, creates the difficulty of localizing, distributing, and maintaining two versions.

Another option is to detect the system and to register the application as a Unicode application on Windows NT/2000 and as an ANSI application on Windows 9x. This may be the best option if you need to run on both Windows 9x and Windows NT/2000, and if you need the broadest possible Unicode support in Windows NT/2000.

For more complete details about these and other options, as well as additional multilingual text support issues in Windows 2000 (formerly Windows NT 5.0), see the article "Supporting Multilanguage Text Layout and Complex Scripts with Windows NT 5.0" in the November 1998 issue of *Microsoft Systems Journal*, available online at www.microsoft.com/msj/1198/multilang/multilangtop.htm.

Tools for adding Unicode support to applications are described later in this chapter.

Backward Compatibility for Non-Unicode Character Sets

Support for Unicode will give users of your application access to text in writing systems for nearly every part of the world—but only if that text was stored in a Unicode-compliant format. If it wasn't, you may need to provide this backward compatibility yourself.

One thing that you don't need to worry about is providing backward compatibility for ASCII. The first 128 values of Unicode match ASCII, making ASCII a kind of direct subset of Unicode, and the commonly used UTF-8 (8-bit) encoding scheme for Unicode represents ASCII characters as themselves.

Another factor is that developers can take advantage of converters that are now available at the OS level for handling conversions to and from Unicode and other character encodings. These converters are discussed later in this chapter, in the *Multilingual Development Aspects of the Major Platforms* section.

Enabling Support for Multibyte Characters and Input Methods

Truly multilingual applications cannot process textual data with the assumption that each character is represented by just one byte. This is an assumption that may be built deeply into text-handling code, and difficult to correct.

To handle multibyte characters, the application's source code must be modified to be aware of multibyte characters, so that operations such as character insertion, deletion, cursor movement and selection, line breaking, copying, pasting, and search-and-replace functions will all work correctly with multibyte characters. As a part of this, allowances must be made for the input method editors (IMEs; also called *front-end processors* [FEPs]) for multibyte characters, which typically require the user to enter paired combinations of keys for each character. The user begins to type the Latin equivalent of a character (phonetically or using some kind of standardized keyboard layout for the language), and the IME compares what the user has typed with a database of patterns. If there is a single match (if one keystroke is used only to produce one particular character, for example), it displays that character. But if there are several matches, as is more likely, the IME waits for the second keystroke that determines the character. Figure 6.1 shows how typing *nihongo* ("Japanese") in the input window for Apple's Japanese Language Kit displays Latin characters as hiragana during entry, which can then be converted to kanji. The hiragana text in the input window produces the kanji text that has already been entered, as shown.

All major platforms have various IMEs available, sometimes several for each language, but naturally an application must be coded to recognize and work with these IMEs so that text input is handled correctly, or that the window used to display character choices does not overwrite a part of the application's user interface, for example.

Practices for Easier Localizability

Wherever possible, elements of the user interface should be isolated from the application's source code in resource files, message files, or databases. This makes it easier to localize these elements in isolation from the source code. In Windows applications, you can do this with resource files or DLLs. For Macintosh applications, use the resource fork. For Java, create a new version of your initial resource bundle for each language. It is also important to be consistent with resource identifiers as a project progresses, so that nothing is overlooked when it comes time to localize.

Don't create text messages dynamically by concatenating strings (linking together words and phrases) to form sentences. Word order usu-

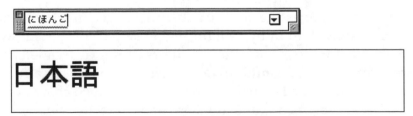

Figure 6.1   The IME for Apple's Japanese Language Kit.

ally varies from language to language, and text messages that are composed dynamically in this way will require code changes to be localized.

On the other hand, it is a good idea to allocate text buffers dynamically because text size may expand when translated. If you have to use static buffers, make them larger than necessary (twice as large as English is one rule of thumb) to make sure there is room for localized strings that may be longer than they are in the source language.

You'll also need to consider exactly how you want to carry out practices for easier localization. Resources can be multilingual, or you can have a separate resource file for each language.

The use of multilingual resources can make things easier because there are fewer resource files to keep track of, but the use of single-language resources makes it easier to change the translations for an individual language, or to add language support by simply adding another new resource. Let the requirements of your project and future plans—such as the possibility of adding more languages in the future—determine which method you use.

User Interface Design

An important aspect of design for applications that will have multilingual interface options or will be localized is allowing for the expansion that may take place when strings for menus, dialog boxes, and other features are localized. Some languages naturally tend to run longer than others, and German, for example, can expand up to about 40 percent over English. Contraction can happen, too, although having too much space is usually less of a problem than not having enough. Figure 6.2 compares the length of the menu bar in QuarkXPress Passport in English, French, German, and Spanish.

The answer, whenever possible, is to leave room for expansion even when coding for the source language. "You only have so much real estate. If you're already pushing it for English, sometimes it can't be helped," says Christopher Hanaoka, director of worldwide research and development for Bowne Global Solutions, "but you should know that either the localized version could be ugly or it's not going to work."

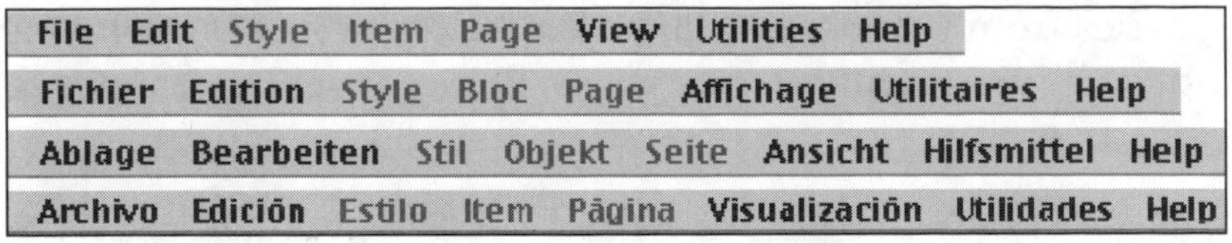

File	Edit	Style	Item	Page	View	Utilities	Help
Fichier	Edition	Style	Bloc	Page	Affichage	Utilitaires	Help
Ablage	Bearbeiten	Stil	Objekt	Seite	Ansicht	Hilfsmittel	Help
Archivo	Edición	Estilo	Item	Página	Visualización	Utilidades	Help

Figure 6.2 The same menu bar can expand by 30 percent or more in localized versions of an application.

It is also a good idea to avoid using text in bitmaps and icons, since these are more difficult to localize than text strings. Once characters have been bitmapped, they are just another part of a graphic file and cannot simply be deleted and retyped the way that they can if they remain text.

Directionality

Not all languages are written from left to right and from top to bottom. Arabic and Hebrew, for example, are *bidirectional* languages because they are written from right to left, but numbers, mathematical expressions, and excerpts from foreign texts are written from left to right. Japanese is frequently written in columns from top to bottom, right to left (literature is typically set vertically, while technical material is set horizontally).

Windows development details on bidirectional Middle Eastern languages are available from the *Microsoft Global Software Development* site at www.microsoft.com/globaldev/mideast/meissues.asp, and for East Asian languages that use vertical text at www.microsoft.com/globaldev/fareast/vertical.asp. For Mac OS details, see the resources listed later in this chapter.

Sorting and Other Character Issues

Even languages that use the Latin alphabet do not always sort from *a* to *z* in the same way as they do in English. For example, in Danish the last letters of the alphabet are *x y z æ ø å*, and in German, the letter *ß* sorts as *ss*. On the other hand, not all languages use only one character to represent a letter. In Spanish, *ch* and *ll* are essentially treated as single letters distinct from the letters *c* and *h* or *l* and *l* (efforts are under-way to change this, but it remains to be seen whether the new method will catch on).

Another character issue occurs in languages such as Chinese, Japanese, and Korean, which do not have upper- and lowercase variants of characters.

Unicode does not address sorting or other semantic issues, but support for these capabilities can be added with development tools, some of which are discussed later in this chapter.

Spacing and Hyphenation

Words in most Asian languages are not separated by spaces, and rules for hyphenation (if it is permitted at all) are complex. Chinese does not hyphenate, while in Japanese, certain characters cannot begin or end a line.

For complete details about text requirements in East Asian languages, see Ken Lunde's comprehensive reference book *CJKV Information Processing* (O'Reilly & Associates, 1999).

Justification is another issue to consider. For example, texts written in the Latin alphabet can be justified (that is, either or both of the left and right edges of the text can be made to line up evenly) by stretching out the spacing between words. In languages that do not have spaces between words, the spacing between characters has to be increased for justification instead.

Calendars

Another issue to keep in mind is calendars, which vary throughout the world. Date formats vary from country to country. Some Middle Eastern countries, for example, use variations on a lunar calendar with months of 29 or 30 days. And (as if Y2K weren't reminder enough to take nothing for granted) years in some calendars do not begin on January 1 and are not numbered from the beginning of the common era.

Details and links to information about other calendars in use world-wide are available at www.panix.com/~wlinden/calendar.shtml.

Multilingual Development Aspects of the Major Platforms

This section offers basic details on multilingual development in Windows, the Mac OS, Java, and Linux, along with pointers to online and print sources of more complete developer information.

Windows

Windows NT has incorporated international support through Unicode character encoding system APIs since its inception, and now this support will be available in all versions of Windows 2000. In addition, new language-specific APIs in Windows 2000 include GetSystemDefaultUILanguage, to get the original language of the system, GetUserDefaultUILanguage, to get the user's language preference, and IsValidLanguageGroup, to check if a particular language group is installed or supported by the user's system. For more details, see www.microsoft.com/globaldev/FAQs/newapis.asp.

The future upgrade path for Windows 98 is still unclear. In early 1999, Microsoft announced a significant Windows 98 update for later in the year, but plans call for eventually including Windows NT technology—and therefore full Unicode support—in consumer versions of Windows, as well.

National Language Support (NLS), which is part of the Microsoft Win32 API, provides a standardized method of supporting multiple international locales, code pages, input methods, and sort orders, as well as number, currency, time, and date formats.

The Win32 NLS API also provides support for Unicode and traditional (pre-Unicode) character sets (such as the Windows ANSI character set) that use 8-bit character values or combinations of 8-bit values to represent the characters used in a specific language or geographical region.

The Win32 NLS API also provides developers with a way to access system-provided Unicode-to-ANSI and ANSI-to-Unicode conversion services, and Windows NT has Extended Binary-Coded Decimal Interchange Code (EBCDIC)-to-Unicode and Unicode-to-EBCDIC translation tables. EBCDIC is an IBM code used on mainframes but generally not on personal computers.

For a more detailed look at NLS in particular, see www.microsoft .com/globaldev/non%20mirror/back%20up/gbl-gen/nlsuppor.htm.

This NLS page is just one part of a much more comprehensive source of globalization issues from Microsoft: the *Going Global* site at www.microsoft.com/globaldev, which provides a wealth of developer information, especially for Windows. The Going Global site provides detailed articles about topics such as globalization, multilanguage text support in Windows 2000, and Unicode, as well as transcripts of Microsoft presentations to global developers, FAQs, links to other Web sites, references, and other sources of information. A page on Windows internationalization design considerations is also available at www.microsoft.com/win32dev/uiguide/uigui445.htm.

Although it has not been updated for several years, an additional source of detailed information for Windows developers that is still well regarded is Nadine Kano's book *Developing International Software for Windows 95 and Windows NT* (Microsoft Press, 1995). Windows 98 in particular has changed relatively little since Windows 95, and so much of the information in this book is still accurate.

Mac OS

The Macintosh held an earlier lead in multilingual computing because of its superior font handling, and Mac OS support for non-Latin writing systems matured in the form of Apple's WorldScript technology, which debuted with System 7.1 in 1993. WorldScript made it possible for developers to provide support for individual or multiple writing systems through a system of scripts. Apple has continued to support WorldScript while bringing support for Unicode to completion in Mac OS 8. An as yet unspecified version of the Mac OS will include a Unicode-based text engine. The next major release, Mac OS X (10), is expected before the end of 1999.

Mac OS capabilities currently available to multilingual developers include: Apple Type Services for Unicode Imaging (ATSUI), which provides display and printing support for Unicode and fully complies with the Unicode Standard version 2.1; Unicode input through the Text Services Manager; and the Text Encoding Converter, which handles conversions to and from Unicode and other text encodings. As shown in Figure 6.3, support for additional encodings can be added by

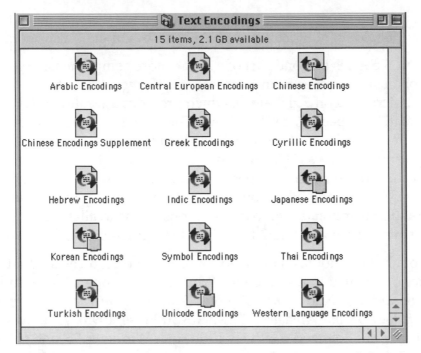

Figure 6.3 Encoding conversions in the Mac OS are supported through plug-ins.

dropping plug-ins into the Text Encodings folder in the Mac OS System Folder.

For full details about the Mac OS Text Encoding Converter, see http://developer.apple.com/techpubs/mac/TextEncodingCMgr/TECRefBook-40.html.

The most general source of information online about Mac OS development is the *Apple Developer* site at www.apple.com/developer. In addition, details about international issues in the Mac OS are available from *Inside Macintosh: Text*, which is available in print (Addison Wesley, 1993) or online at http://developer.apple.com/techpubs/mac/Text/Text-2.html. This resource has become somewhat dated since the release of Mac OS 8 in 1997, but it still contains useful reference information.

Few details are currently available about Mac OS X, but go to http://developer.apple.com/macos to download the white paper "Transitioning to Mac OS X." This developer-oriented document has a section called "Text and Other International Services" which details updates for OS X about technologies such as the Script Manager, Text Utilities, Font Manager, and others.

Java

By its nature as a cross-platform technology that can be used anywhere it is supported, Java offers developers a variety of multilingual and international features that have been added to traditional platforms as an afterthought. Java includes full native support for Unicode and converters for handling non-Unicode text, the ability to isolate translatable text in resource bundles, and a variety of classes for dealing with locale-specific data such as numbers, currencies, dates, and times.

Online lessons in Java internationalization are available from Sun Microsystems at http://java.sun.com/docs/books/tutorial/i18n/index.html. This site includes sample programs, an explanation of setting locales, and methods for isolating locale-specific data, formatting numbers, dates, and text messages according to locale, and working with text independently of locale.

Linux

Support for multilingual development in Linux, the open-source implementation of Unix, is still something of a work in progress. The Linux kernel itself supports Unicode and lends itself well to multilingual development, but many Linux utilities and applications are still limited to the Latin alphabet by the availability of fonts and input methods.

APIs for handling locale-specific issues such as character sets, date formats, and so forth in Linux (and other Unix variants) have been specified by the Portable Operating System Interface for Unix (POSIX). Details are available from the ISO POSIX home page (http://anubis .dkuug.dk/JTC1/SC22/WG15/) and the Portable Application Standards Committee (www.pasc.org).

A detailed look at Linux internationalization is provided by Stephen Turnbull's article "Alphabet Soup: The Internationalization of Linux" in the March 1999 issue of *Linux Journal*, available online at www.ssc .com/lj/issue59/3286.html. The article delves into internationalization and the Linux kernel, file systems, text input and display, and other issues.

For further details about support for Unicode in Linux, see the *Linux Complete Command Reference* (SAMS Publishing, 1997), particularly pages 1253 to 1256.

Development Tools

A wide variety of environments and tools are available for multilingual development. Before looking at the specifics of these products, it is helpful to consider how to pick one that is appropriate for your work.

Wes Nakamura, a software localizer, advises keeping the following things in mind when choosing environments and tools for multilingual development.

Target. Some tools are targeted at developers who have to write code for multiple languages which they may not speak. These tend to deal with functionality in a way that is relatively removed from the language itself. Others are targeted at translators to help deal with resource files that must be translated, and still others are designed to help programmers and translators work together more smoothly.

The vendor. It's important to ask whether the product's vendor will respond to bugs you find, continue to support the platforms you need, and make changes to customize the software for your purposes. If the vendor is unable or unwilling to do this, will you be able to get source code for custom changes to the development tool?

Capabilities. Does the tool allow you to expand? For example, you may now be working only in single-byte languages, but you may need to provide for multibyte capabilities in the future. "It's quite often that you suddenly realize you want to add a feature that you considered originally but decided was unnecessary. By going with fuller capabilities you can save a lot of headaches later."

Translators. If translators will need to use the tool (for example, to translate resource files) is it easy for them to use? "If using the software is cumbersome and keeps their attention off the translation itself, that's obviously not a good thing, even if the software does help the programmer."

Preexisting software. If you want to localize a piece of preexisting software, does the tool require you to use special formats (for example, for localizing text strings) that are incompatible with what you already have? An ideal tool will be compatible with the work you have already done.

With these considerations in mind, the following development environments and tools may be helpful in developing multilingual applications.

Batam Internationalization Library

The internationalization libraries of Batam, from Alis Technologies (www.alis.com), make it possible to add multilingual support to existing Windows applications. Based on Unicode, Batam's functionality includes the ability to add character-set converters, input functions, multilingual display functions, and support for language-dependent processes such as line breaking and hyphenation.

Developer's Kit for Unicode

The Developer's Kit for Unicode (UDK), from Sybase (www.sybase .com), provides tools for developers to create multilingual applications using Unilib, a library of Unicode string- and character-manipulation and conversion routines. UDK is compatible with version 2.1 of the Unicode Standard and supports more than 90 character-set conversions, as well as Unicode multilingual data sorting using Unilib sorting routines. Also bundled with the UDK is *MLQuery* (www.starglobe .com), a multilingual query tool to display, input, and query multilingual data, along with test data for 25 languages and a WorldType Unicode font to use in debugging Unicode applications.

Flores Toolkit

Flores, from Alis Technologies (www.alis.com), is an internationalization engineering toolkit for adding linguistic capabilities to an application, operating system, or electronic device. Libraries that can be called by C or C++ are available for capabilities such as the identification of character encodings; line breaking, hyphenation, and word extraction for non-Latin text; and Asian language input. Ready-made versions of Flores are available for Windows and Solaris, but versions for other platforms are available on a custom basis.

Global C

Global C, from Uniscape (www.uniscape.com), is a multilingual, multiplatform (PC and Unix) API and runtime library that enables development of single-source-code applications that work anywhere in the world. Global C allows applications to support Unicode, even on operating systems without Unicode support. Features include a locale-definition utility, multibyte-enabled string-manipulation and locale-sensitive data-formatting functions, support for the major European and Asian languages, and backward compatibility with legacy data such as non-Unicode-compliant applications and data.

Global C is especially useful for cross-platform development for Windows and Unix because it acts as a universal localization API, which allows you to keep a single source base instead of having branches for each platform. Its basis in C also makes it well suited for expanding from software that runs only on Unix servers, by providing Windows clients, for example.

ProVoice and PrimoVOX

ProVoice and PrimoVOX, from First Byte (www.fbyte.com), allow developers to include text-to-speech capabilities and synthesized speech output in their Windows applications (support for other platforms is said to be in the works). Using First Byte's SpeechFont technology, language variations can be added as well, such as voices for U.S. or U.K. English, or Spanish, French, German, and Italian voices. In addition, ProVoice can be synchronized with animated graphics, such as a bouncing ball that highlights the text being spoken.

PassWord

Spell-checking support for various languages can be added to applications for Windows, Macintosh, Unix and other platforms with PassWord, from Circle Noetic Services (www.mv.com/ipusers/noetic/password.html). PassWord requires as little as 50K of RAM to operate and is written in portable C code that uses a single engine for all languages. PassWord can add spell-checking for the major Western European languages, as well as Russian and Arabic.

PolyGlot

PolyGlot, from Pretty Objects Computers (www.prettyobjects.com), enables developers to determine what needs to be changed to present their applications in other languages using a single source code. Using Delphi or C++ Builder, developers can prepare for translations by exporting all character strings to a table and reimporting them after translation. PolyGlot can also help manage multilingual elements such as help files, date and numerical formats, and Windows dialog boxes, and can generate applications that permit users to switch from one language to another at runtime.

PowerBuilder

The Sybase PowerBuilder (www.sybase.com/products/powerbuilder) Enterprise application development tool has multilingual features such as support for Unicode, and the ability to merge Japanese double-byte character support into the ANSI PowerBuilder common code-base. Hebrew- and Arabic-enabled 32-bit versions of PowerBuilder offer right-to-left support, and versions of PowerBuilder localized deployment kits make it easier to deploy PowerBuilder applications with standard run-time dialog boxes and error messages in eight European languages (Danish, Dutch, French, German, Italian, Norwegian, Spanish, and Swedish).

PowerBuilder Enterprise for Unicode supports UTF-16, and Unicode PowerBuilder applications can be deployed only as 32-bit applications on Windows NT. Only two databases, Sybase SQL and Oracle, are currently supported in the Unicode version, but PowerBuilder for Unicode generates Unicode HTML, meaning that browsers that support Unicode (such as versions 4 and higher of Microsoft Internet Explorer and Netscape Navigator) can read it.

Rosette

Basic Technology's Rosette (www.basistech.com/products) is a C++ source-code library for working in Unicode and other text encodings used in legacy character sets. Designed to enable developers to quickly add Unicode compliance to their products, Rosette is portable to Windows, Macintosh, and Unix applications. Rosette is commonly embedded into applications and used to convert text from external sources into Unicode.

SSA-NAME3

SSA-NAME3, from Search Software America (www.searchsoftware
.com/ssaprod.htm), is a software toolset for developers of applications
that require advanced search and matching capabilities on names
of people, companies, titles, and other short descriptive texts. SSA-
NAME3's Language & Country Support allows work with data from
more than 40 countries using either the local script or Latinized
versions.

TX Text Control

The TX Text Control development tool, from Griffin Technologies
(www.griftech.com/html/Tx.htm), allows the addition of support for
Unicode, and provides built-in support for English, German, Spanish,
French, Italian, and Japanese, in addition to other text control. TX Text
Control supports environments including VisualBasic, Delphi, Visual
C++, Borland C++, PowerBuilder, Visual FoxPro, and Microsoft Access.

Another Griffin product, CheckMate (www.griftech.com/html/cmate
.htm), allows the addition of spelling dictionaries for U.S. and U.K.
English, as well as French, Spanish, and German.

VisualBasic

Recent versions of Microsoft VisualBasic (http://msdn.microsoft
.com/vbasic) have introduced resource files, which simplify international development. Win32 resources can be used in different development environments and on different platforms (such as Windows or
Java), which minimizes the effort required for localization by allowing the reuse of translations. A small set of localization tools, such as
VisualBasic Language Manager Pro (www.whippleware.com), can now
be used for a variety of products.

WinMASS 2000 SDK

WinMASS 2000, from Star+Globe (www.starglobe.com), is a multilanguage enabling system for the English Windows environment. Win-
MASS 2000 has capabilities for end users (reading, creating, editing,
and printing documents in Simplified and Traditional Chinese, Japanese, Korean, and Tamil, as well as European languages), but its soft-

ware development kit allows developers to enable their programs with multilingual capabilities by integrating routines for Unicode, the WinMASS environment, and code conversion. WinMASS 2000 supports double-byte character sets and the Unicode standard (UTF-7 and UTF-8), and conversion between encodings such as Simplified Chinese (GB2312-80) and Traditional Chinese (Big5).

Other Tools

While not development tools per se, the following tools can help to check code for possible international problems or to create multilingual installers.

Global Checker for C/C++ and Java

Global Checker, also from Uniscape (www.uniscape-inc.com/products/c_java_features.shtml), runs under Windows 9x or NT 4.0 and automatically checks code to isolate multilingual support problems, such as ensuring that string-related function calls are multibyte-enabled, scanning for and reporting any code that is noncompliant under NLS standards, and identifying hard-coded strings to streamline the localization process.

Global Checker for Java provides a way to move hard-coded strings to ResourceBundle files and allows users to read existing ResourceBundle files and add new messages.

There is also an HTML-formatted *Global Primer* that suggests development solutions to globalization problems. Once an error or a potential problem has been identified, the Global Primer can be checked for options to correct the problem. Some developers use this as a way to learn about globalization issues at their own pace.

I18n Expeditor and I18n Reporter

I18n Expeditor, from OneRealm, Inc. (www.onerealm.com), is a source-code analysis tool that detects internationalization problems such as hard-coded text and locale-specific functions. It can automatically perform the necessary corrections and updates, or provide recommendations on how to solve problems. It also offers statistics for assessing the code's international readiness.

I18n Reporter is a command-line assessment tool that can be incorporated into scripts or batch processes to find internationalization problems, providing summary reports which can then be corrected using I18n Expeditor.

C and C++ versions of both products are available, and a Java version is in development.

InstallShield

InstallShield International (www.installshield.com) enables Windows and Java developers to create multilingual installers in 30 languages. As shown in Figure 6.4, the InstallShield environment visually organizes application, setup, and help files, making it easier to build one installation that targets all the languages you support, or to build a separate installer for each language. InstallShield International has East and West versions, which include the 8 major Asian languages plus Russian and 22 European languages, respectively. A related prod-

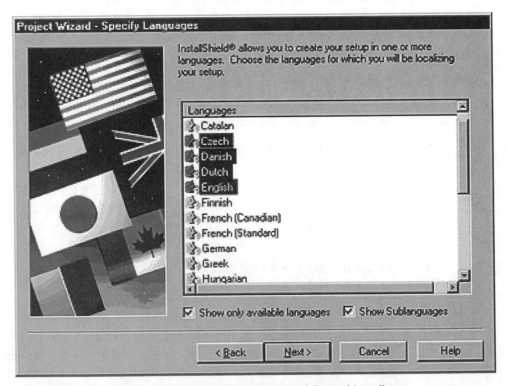

Figure 6.4 InstallShield International helps build multilingual installers.

uct, *DemoShield*, allows the creation of demo versions of applications in 30 languages. Language-specific resources are stored in designated folders, so that when a demo is run, it detects the language of the user's system and uses the appropriate resources.

Other Resources

For further information about multilingual development details and tools, consult the following sources.

Books

For an in-depth and highly regarded look at how to handle the major East Asian languages (Chinese, Japanese, Korean, and Vietnamese), see Ken Lunde's *CJKV Information Processing* (O'Reilly & Associates, 1999).

An excellent and up-to-date listing of books about internationalization and other multilingual development issues is available through the site for *MultiLingual Computing & Technology* magazine, at www .multilingual.com.

Resources for multilingual development for the Mac OS are provided by the International Macintosh Users Group (www.imug.org).

Conferences

The International Unicode Conference, sponsored by the World Wide Web Consortium and other organizations, is held twice each year, generally once in San Jose, California, and once in another city. The conference is intended for developers and users of Unicode software. For more information, check the Web site for the fifteenth conference, held August 30 to September 2, 1999 (the most current conference planned as of this writing), at www.reuters.com/unicode/iuc15.

Courses

Courses specifically on software internationalization are available at some schools (but a surprisingly limited number), such as a course offered in 1999 at the University of California Santa Cruz extension called "Microsoft Windows 95/NT Internationalization." This course covers topics such as international character sets and code pages, Unicode, the Win32 National Language Support API, and internationalization support in C and C++.

Also available in the Silicon Valley area is a one-day course in Java internationalization from Vivid Solutions. See www.vivids.com for more details.

Next

The development of multilingual applications isn't only a coding issue. It is sometimes necessary to create additional language resources, such as keyboards and fonts, or to convert legacy data stored in different character encodings. These issues are examined in the next chapter.

CHAPTER 7

Creating and Converting Multilingual Resources

Naturally, it is usually easiest and best (for the sake of compatibility) to use existing language solutions that follow agreed-upon standards.

This chapter covers what you can do when using existing solutions is not possible.

Although it is becoming less and less likely, sometimes a resource that you need—a font, for example—simply may not exist for a particular language. Or even if one does exist, a language resource such as a font may suffer from a number of drawbacks. It might lack unique characters that you need, such as a scientific symbol or a historical character that is no longer in common use. Or, the fonts that exist for your language might lack the appearance and style that you want, or you might simply want to create these resources in-house so that you own all the rights to them and can use and distribute them without worrying about copyright issues and licensing fees.

This chapter discusses how to create multilingual resources, such as keyboard layouts and fonts, as well as how to do conversions from one encoding to another.

Creating Multilingual Resources

At the outset of this chapter, the importance of avoiding hacked solutions can't be stressed enough. This is particularly true of fonts, because work created in nonstandard fonts may have to be converted in the future.

If a solution for what you need doesn't already exist, it is well worth the trouble to at least make sure that any resources that you create are as compliant as possible with Unicode or any other relevant standards. As Andrea Vine, an internationalization architect at Sun Microsystems, says, "It's never wrong to choose a standard over a proprietary set."

For example, when designing a new font for a writing system that is already a part of the Unicode standard, put the new font's characters in the same order and use the same code points as another Unicode-compliant font for the same language (the tools described later in this chapter can give you a look inside the fonts you already have). If you are modifying a font by simply adding a few characters that the font does not include, check the Unicode Consortium's code charts (http://charts.unicode.org/charts.html) to see if the Unicode standard already includes your characters. If it does, then you can put your version of the character in the appropriate position within the font you are modifying.

If you are dealing with characters (or entire writing systems) that have not been included in the Unicode standard at this point, you have more freedom to do what you want. It may still make sense, however, to make your resources comply to any other existing standards for them, such as a commonly used national encoding for the languages you need to work with. If the characters for these languages are eventually included in Unicode, conforming to an existing standard may make conversion significantly easier.

Conforming to standards whenever possible—ideally to Unicode, but to other relevant standards as necessary—is the best and most basic way to avoid future confusion and incompatibility with multilingual texts.

Custom Keyboards

Fortunately, compatibility issues are less important when dealing with resources such as user-defined keyboards. This is because content is independent of the keyboard layout used to enter it (in English, for example, it makes no difference in the text you type whether you type it with a QWERTY keyboard or a Dvorak keyboard, or use voice-recognition software). This means that you are relatively free to design new keyboard layouts as needed.

The question is whether this is necessary. Except in rare cases, it is unlikely that a keyboard that you may need doesn't already exist. See the suggestions in the *Computing Support for Other World Languages and Language Groups* section of Chapter 1, "The World-Ready Computer," for online directories of fonts, keyboards, and other language resources.

When it is necessary, you can create your own unique keyboard layout, but this can cause you trouble in the future if you aren't careful. For example, if you create a custom keyboard that puts the characters for your language in nonstandard positions, and you then spend several years typing with this keyboard layout, it can be frustrating to learn a new keyboard if you need to make a switch at some time in the future, or if you simply need to use someone else's computer. In the 1980s, for example, several slightly differing keyboard layouts came into use for Russian. Many of the characters in the Cyrillic alphabet correspond closely to Latin letters and can be naturally matched up on a standard U.S. English keyboard, but others aren't such an easy match and were placed somewhat arbitrarily. In the 1990s, however, standardized keyboard layouts began to come into wider use and users had to readjust. Learning to type with a new keyboard layout in this way isn't an insurmountable difficulty, but it has been a source of frustration for many multilingual users. Now that standards are in place for most languages, the frustration that can be caused by using a hacked keyboard layout is best avoided.

When you do need or want to create your own custom keyboard layout, however, there are a few Windows and Macintosh options.

Creating Custom Keyboards in Windows

One option for creating a custom keyboard layout to make typing in a particular language easier for you is *3-D Keyboard,* from Fingertip Software (www.fingertipsoft.com). This application offers several preconfigured keyboard layouts for common Western European languages, but, as shown in Figure 7.1, 3-D Keyboard also allows you to create custom keyboard layouts for any other languages that use the Latin alphabet.

To do this, you simply drag and drop characters onto the image of the keyboard. While 3-D Keyboard is running, whatever keyboard layout you have selected will be the layout that is used for any typing you do in other applications. You can minimize the 3-D Keyboard window to keep it out of your way while using it.

Another well-regarded and more versatile option for creating custom keyboard layouts is a $15 shareware application (free for noncommercial use) called *Janko's Keyboard Generator* (http://solair.eunet.yu/~janko/engdload.htm). As shown in Figure 7.2, Janko's Keyboard Generator is similar to 3-D Keyboard. You can create custom keyboard lay-

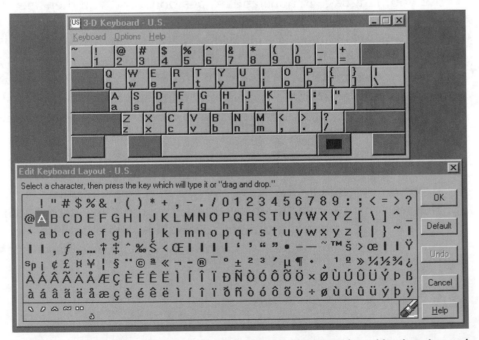

Figure 7.1 You can create custom Latin keyboards in 3-D Keyboard by dragging and dropping the characters you want.

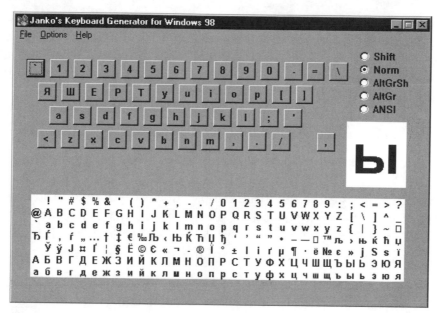

Figure 7.2 Creating a custom Cyrillic keyboard in Janko's Keyboard Generator.

outs for any languages that use the Latin or Cyrillic alphabets. To do it, you drag and drop characters to the application's keyboard image.

Unlike 3-D Keyboard, however, Janko's Keyboard Generator gives you a choice of several modes besides normal (lowercase) and shift (uppercase). You can also set up key combinations using the Alt and other keys.

After you've set up your keyboard, you can save it as a .kbd file and place it in the Windows System folder to replace the keyboard there or to serve as one of several keyboard options.

Creating Custom Keyboards in Mac OS

Apple's freeware Macintosh resource-editing application *ResEdit* allows you to open and edit system resources such as keyboard layouts. By modifying a copy of an existing keyboard layout, you can essentially create your own custom version.

NOTE

It is important to always work with copies in ResEdit, so you don't damage or destroy your originals.

When editing a keyboard layout, as shown in Figure 7.3, ResEdit displays all the characters that are available for a particular font in the upper matrix. In the lower portion of the window, Tables 0 to 9 show the characters that are produced when typed in combination with a particular key. *Table 3* in Figure 7.3 shows the characters that are produced when typed in combination with the Option key in the font Palatino CE, using a keyboard designed for Czech called *Czech-U.S.*

To modify a keyboard layout, you simply drag characters from the top of the ResEdit window and drop them into the desired position on the keyboard image at the bottom. For example, if you want the key combination Option-q to produce a particular character in your new keyboard layout, hold down the Option key in ResEdit and drag and drop the desired letter to the position of the letter *q*.

Before saving your new keyboard layout, go to the Resource menu and choose Get Resource Info, shown in Figure 7.4. In this window, change the name of this keyboard layout and assign a new ID number. You may want to open copies of the other keyboard layouts you use to

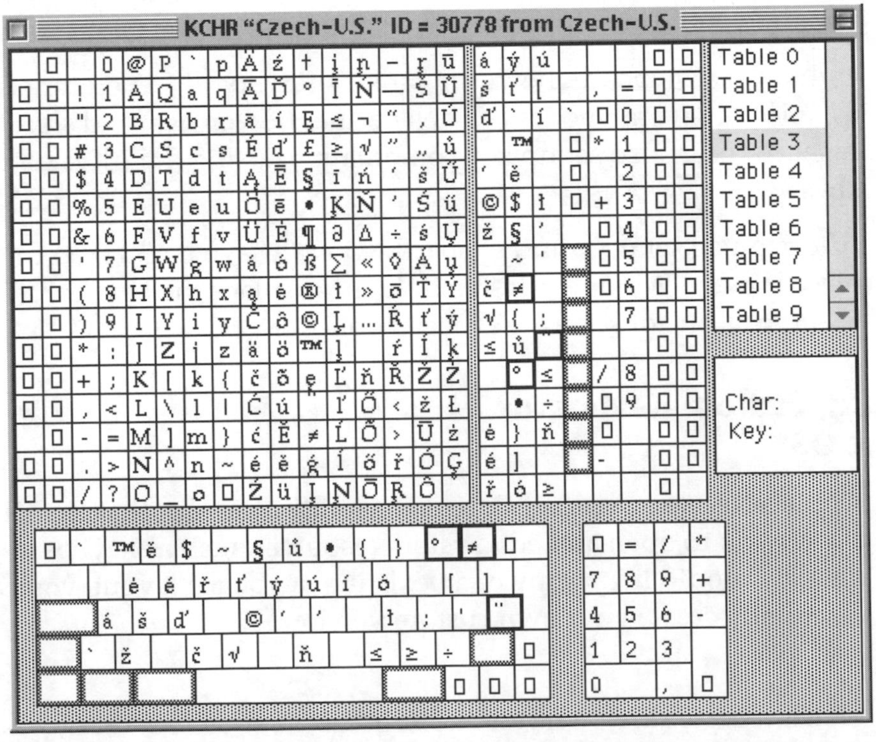

Figure 7.3 ResEdit allows the creation of custom Mac keyboard layouts.

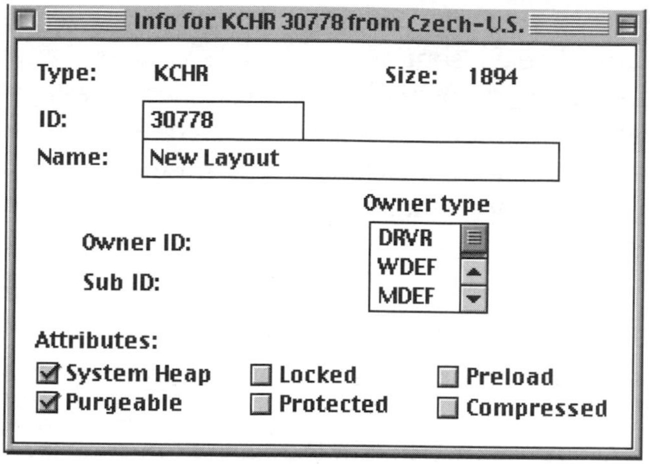

```
┌──────────────────────────────────────────────────┐
│ □ ═══  Info for KCHR 30778 from Czech-U.S. ═══ ▤  │
│ ┌────────────────────────────────────────────┐   │
│ │ Type:     KCHR           Size:   1894        │   │
│ │                                              │   │
│ │ ID:    ┌──────────────┐                      │   │
│ │        │ 30778        │                      │   │
│ │ Name:  ┌──────────────────────────────┐     │   │
│ │        │ New Layout                   │     │   │
│ │                                              │   │
│ │                        Owner type            │   │
│ │     Owner ID:          ┌──────────┐          │   │
│ │                        │ DRVR   ▤ │          │   │
│ │     Sub ID:            │ WDEF   ▲ │          │   │
│ │                        │ MDEF   ▼ │          │   │
│ │                        └──────────┘          │   │
│ │ Attributes:                                  │   │
│ │ ☑ System Heap   ☐ Locked      ☐ Preload      │   │
│ │ ☑ Purgeable     ☐ Protected   ☐ Compressed   │   │
│ └────────────────────────────────────────────┘   │
└──────────────────────────────────────────────────┘
```

Figure 7.4 ResEdit's resource information window.

check their ID numbers and make sure that you don't assign one of their numbers to your new layout. Because of the way the Mac OS handles keyboard layouts, it is a good idea to assign your new layout a number that is simply its previous number plus 1, so that it stays within the same range for the script you are creating it for. For a more precise guidance in assigning an ID number, see the Mac OS script code and resource ID ranges available online at http://developer .apple.com/techpubs/mac/Text/Text-534.html#HEADING534-0. You may also benefit from reading Appendix B of *Inside Macintosh: Text* available at http://developer.apple.com/techpubs/mac/Text/ Text-531.html, which offers specific details about keyboards and other international resources.

ResEdit is an unsupported application, but for more details see Derrick Schneider's book *Zen and the Art of Resource Editing* (Hayden Books, 1995) or Peter Alley and Carolyn Strange's *ResEdit Complete* (Addison-Wesley, 1994).

Unfortunately, another popular Macintosh resource editor, *Resorceror,* does not have a dedicated keyboard editor at this time.

Fonts

Most of the world's languages are already handled by existing fonts, and so before you go and create a new one (or even just a few special characters for one) it is worth making sure that an easily available solution doesn't already exist somewhere. Unless you need a font that you or your organization will own all the rights to, or unless you need a font with special typographic characteristics, such as a particular style, you may be able to find a Unicode-compliant font for the language (or languages) you need that contains all the characters you need. And even if you find a font that doesn't contain every character you need but is close, it may be easiest to simply modify this font instead of starting from scratch.

Sources of fonts—including companies like Monotype (www .monotype.com) that design fonts primarily for original equipment manufacturer (OEM) sale—are listed in the *Computing Support for Other World Languages and Language Groups* section of Chapter 1. Look there first for a font that fits your needs.

If you can't find one, read on.

Creating and Modifying Fonts

If you need only a few characters, it may make the most sense to simply add them to an existing font. When doing this, be sure to design whatever new characters that you need in the same typographical style (keeping in mind that styles may be locale-dependent) as the rest of the font to which you want to add the character. A relatively easy way to do this is to assemble the new character using parts of existing characters in the font you are modifying.

A situation in which you might want to create an entirely new font is if you need a font for a seldom-used or dead language, or for a fictional language in an entertainment product (extensive work has gone into fonts for Klingon and D'Ni, languages from *Star Trek* and the game Riven). You might also want to do this if you need to own all the rights to a font to be able to distribute it without paying royalties, or you might have specific style requirements for a font that you can't get in any fonts that are commercially available for your script. There are two main options for creating and modifying fonts to suit your needs. *Fontographer* and *FontLab/FontLab Composer* can handle the job of creating entire fonts and can also make this work easier by importing characters that have been created in digital graphics formats, such as EPS, or scans of fonts from existing print sources, such as from an old book or manuscript.

EuroFonter

EuroFonter, from Pyrus N.A. (www.pyrus.com), is a product designed for adding one specific character to your fonts: the euro symbol. Euro-Fonter allows you to add a euro symbol to any font that you select. As shown in Figure 7.5, EuroFonter allows you to build a euro character for each font in ways that ensure that it will match the rest of your font, such as building it by combining the C character and a set of euro double-bar characters. EuroFonter also lets you decide where in your fonts to place the new character, as well as the key combination for typing it.

Fontographer

One tool for font creation and editing is Macromedia Fontographer (www.macromedia.com/software/fontographer), which allows you to modify existing Type 1, Type 3, and TrueType fonts, or create an entirely new typeface. Fontographer can be used to create fonts for Windows, Macintosh, NeXT, and Solaris, and Fontographer itself is available for both the Mac and the PC. Figure 7.6 shows a Devanagari

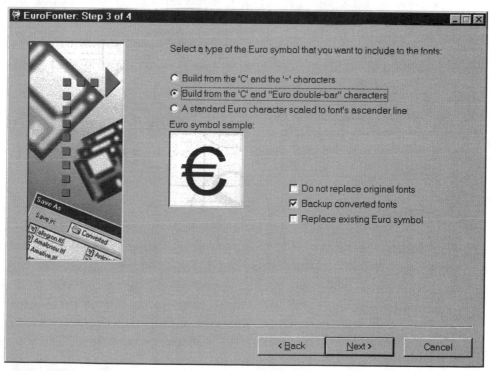

Figure 7.5   EuroFonter can create a euro symbol based on a font's C character.

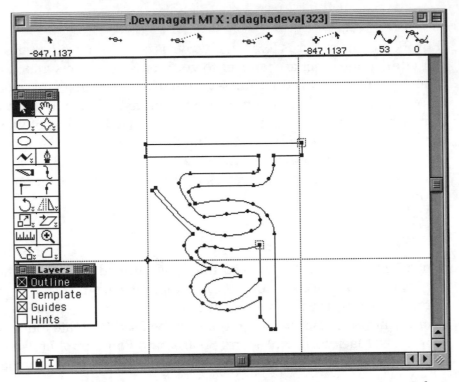

Figure 7.6 Fontographer allows you to modify existing fonts or create new fonts.

character in Fontographer's outline window. Fontographer provides detailed control over the appearance, spacing, and other qualities of the characters that make up a font.

Although it is widely considered the industry standard, Fontographer has one drawback: It has not been significantly revised since 1994, and there is some uncertainty about the product's future and Macromedia's commitment to it.

FontLab

Another option is FontLab, from Pyrus N.A. (www.pyrus.com), which allows you to create PC Type 1 and PC TrueType fonts with Unicode and other encodings.

FontLab can only create PC fonts, but another Pyrus product, TransType, can convert PC fonts to Macintosh format. In addition to allowing conversions to and from Mac and PC formats, as shown in Figure 7.7, TransType can also deal with a variety of international encodings, such as Unicode and ANSI.

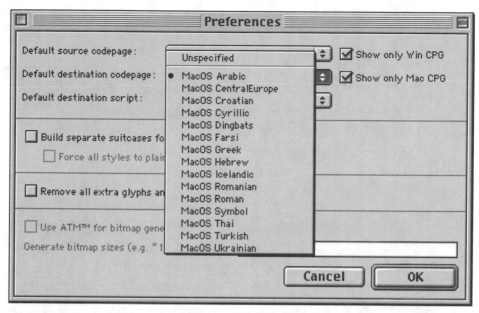

Figure 7.7 TransType handles a range of default source codepage conversions.

Figure 7.8 illustrates one of FontLab's advantages over Fontographer—an extensive set of built-in font-creation *templates* for many writing systems and encodings, such as Unicode.

Another related Pyrus product, *FontLab Composer*, is designed specifically for fonts that have more than 1,000 characters, such as fonts for East Asian languages, or fonts that used to contain characters for several scripts, such as a font that includes characters for the Latin, Hebrew, Cyrillic, and Arabic writing systems. FontLab Composer's internal font manager also lets you combine characters from several existing fonts into a single composite font.

Composer also allows you to export fonts in a format called *CID* (formally known as *CID-Keyed Fonts Format*), which was developed by Adobe Systems to simplify the creation of international fonts—specifically Chinese, Japanese, and Korean. CID fonts are essentially Type 1 fonts and can generally be used with PostScript devices.

Demo versions of all three of these Pyrus products are available through the Pyrus N.A. Web site at www.pyrus.com, and Pyrus also makes available a list of links to other freeware and shareware font utilities that are available from other companies.

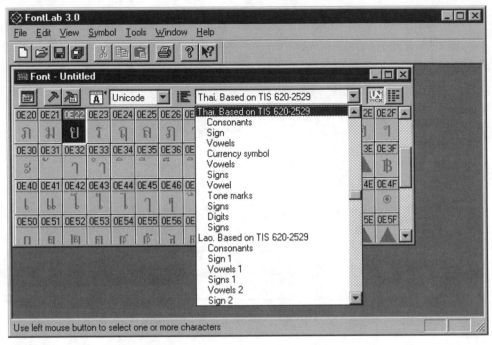

Figure 7.8 Choosing a font-creation template in FontLab.

Other Font Techniques

Creating your own double-byte font should be approached with caution. Even creating a new font for the Latin alphabet with 100 or 200 characters can be time-consuming, and it can be very difficult to create the large number of characters needed for East Asian languages. In this case, you may want to reconsider starting with an existing font. You may be able to create the characters you need by modifying copies of existing characters that are similar, if they are available.

There are a few different options for how to include newly created characters. You can add them to your old font, save them separately in a different font file that contains only your new characters, or save them as a completely new font file containing all the old and new characters. "Your own workflow should indicate what a suitable procedure would be," says Dirk Meyer, a CJKV font developer for Adobe Systems.

If possible, give your characters the same encodings they have in Unicode to ensure future compatibility. Otherwise, if a Unicode-compliant font that includes the characters you need becomes available in the future, your custom characters will render as null characters, or, worse, they may occupy the positions of other needed characters.

Another issue to keep in mind when designing new characters is how to make them accessible. "If it is a CJK character, the question is: can you customize your input method in order to accommodate input strings for user-defined characters," says Meyer, "or can you get it through a single keystroke? Again, your working environment should suggest the approach."

It is also important to keep copyright issues in mind. Modifying fonts that you own (or that are in the public domain) isn't a problem, but reselling them or distributing unlicensed copies of them is illegal. Like other software, many fonts are copyrighted and cannot be freely distributed.

Getting Outside Help with Custom Font Design

Designing custom fonts isn't easy, and although it is possible to do it yourself with some of the tools described in this chapter, you may want to have professionals do it for you.

The following design firms can do font work in non-Latin alphabets.

Galápagos Design Group (http://galapagosdesign.com). Developers of a wide variety of non-Latin fonts for languages and alphabets including Arabic, Chinese, Cyrillic, Devanagari, Japanese, Laotian, and Thai. Galápagos designed the kanji fonts that shipped with Apple's OS 7.0J, and also developed Cyrillic fonts for Lockheed Martin for use in a joint U.S.-Russian space project.

Monotype Typography (www.monotype.com). Specializes in creating modules of fonts and scripts for a customer's required language support and can handle nearly all of the world's writing systems. Most of Monotype's clients are OEMs, including some of the most prominent companies in the computer industry: Microsoft, IBM, Apple, and Sun.

ParaType, Inc. (www.paratype.com). Specializes in Cyrillic fonts, but has also done work for Latin-alphabet languages, Arabic, Greek, Hebrew, and others. ParaType has designed Cyrillic fonts used for Russian currency and the Russian edition of *PC Magazine*. ParaType's office is in Moscow.

Tiro Typeworks (www.tiro.com). Offers both Latin and non-Latin scripts. Tiro's non-Latin specialty is Cyrillic, but the company recently has begun branching out into work in languages including Greek, Armenian, Georgian, and others. Tiro's list of clients includes Microsoft, Linotype Library GmbH, and Agfa. Tiro Typeworks is based in Vancouver.

What should you expect when approaching a company about designing a font? John Hudson, a type designer and cofounder of Tiro Typeworks, says it's not unusual for prospective clients not to know what's involved at first. "Often, clients do not have the technical vocabulary to talk about their needs, so education is the first part of our job. The initial brief can be as simple as 'We need a font for Vietnamese' and we need to discern what font format they will require, what platforms they need to ship to, whether they need the font to be optimized for onscreen legibility, and which Vietnamese encoding is going to work best for them."

"We also encourage clients to think in the long term," Hudson says. "A custom font can be a significant investment, particularly if it is optimized for screen, which requires many hours of manual editing, so it is important to get as much value from a font as possible. This usually involves looking at your future plans and considering how your font requirements might change as, for instance, your business expands into new markets."

Determining Whether Unicode Includes a Character You Need

The Unicode Consortium publishes code charts for the current Unicode standard, as well as details about additional scripts and characters that are currently under consideration. These details are available online (www.unicode.org) and in print (*The Unicode Standard: Version 2.0*, Addison-Wesley, 1996).

Looking through the code charts for the Unicode standard for a character that you need, it is important to keep in mind that Unicode is organized by *scripts*, not languages, in order to avoid duplication. Dozens of languages all share the Latin letter *a*, for example, and so it is included only once. The same is true for other scripts that support multiple languages, such as Cyrillic and Han characters (Chinese, Japanese, and Korean). Keep in mind, however, that it can be difficult to determine if one character used in Japan is really identical to a very similar one that is used in China. There are rules for handling closely-related variants like these in the Unicode standard.

Unicode also has separate charts for diacritical marks, punctuation, mathematical operators, and a variety of other characters and symbols.

Conversions

At some point, in spite of all your best-laid plans, you'll probably need to convert documents created with one character set to another. You may need to do this in order to share multilingual documents with someone who uses a different character set from your own (the documents you send back and forth may end up looking like some kind of interplanetary code), or you may need to open and use older documents that were created before you settled on your current standard.

This section deals with relatively small case-by-case conversions that you might need to do on the fly, as well as larger projects, such as converting a large amount of legacy data.

Font-to-Font Conversions

Switching from one font to another, even across platforms, is usually no problem, as long as these fonts use the same character encoding. When you switch from Arial to Times New Roman, for instance, text in any Western European language shouldn't change, because both fonts were designed with the same character encoding in mind.

Unfortunately, however, some fonts have been designed with no particular encoding in mind and simply have characters mapped (often phonetically) onto the characters of the ASCII character set: The *a* key might type the phonetic equivalent of *a* in another language in the font you are using.

Since the 26 letters of a standard English keyboard can't accommodate all the characters and sounds of some other languages, however, the characters that don't fit may be typed with other keys or key combinations that are more or less arbitrary. For example, there is unfortunately a profusion of Russian fonts in which only about 80 percent of

Script Unification

If you have found a character (or script) that has definitely not yet been included in Unicode, you might want to start by proposing its inclusion in a future version of the Unicode standard. Details about how to do this are available online at www.unicode.org/pending/proposals.html. Proposals must be made in writing and should include an image of any proposed characters, as well as a justification for their inclusion. And if you are particularly interested in Han characters, you may want to contact the Ideographic Rapporteur Group (www.cse.cuhk.edu.hk/~irg), which works to ensure that needed Han characters are included.

"This process of including your new character into Unicode takes time," warns Meyer. "You certainly don't want to wait until the inclusion process by the official standards bodies is finished." What, then, can you do in the meantime?

According to Meyer, if your character is already included in Unicode, then you can modify or create a font that includes the character with this encoding (see the earlier section, *Creating and Modifying Fonts*). If not, Meyer says it can be helpful to ask where the character comes from. "There are some non-Unicode character collections out there that suggest a code assignment which is close, or better, identical, to the original source." In other words, if at all possible, put this character in a position where it will match its position in the original source (a commonly used national encoding, for example) for the sake of easier conversions.

There are also some well-established mappings for certain code points in Unicode's Private Use Area. Although the characters used by these code points are not officially part of the Unicode Standard at this point, conventions have emerged. It may be to your advantage to base your own work on these mappings. For more details about these mappings, see the mapping tables that are available from the Unicode Consortium at http://charts.unicode.org/charts.html or ftp://ftp.unicode.org. For East Asian languages, see Appendix Q, "Character Codes and Mapping Tables," in Ken Lunde's book *CJKV Information Processing* (O'Reilly & Associates, 1999).

"If the character is completely new," Meyer says, "you can use your own inspiration or requirements as to where in the encoding range to place this character." In particular, you may want to consider putting your character in the user-defined Private Use Area of Unicode. The Private Use Area is divided into several subareas, one of which is an End User Subarea.

As shown in Figure 7.9, the application Fontographer allows you to view and sort your fonts by a variety of characteristics, including their Unicode values.

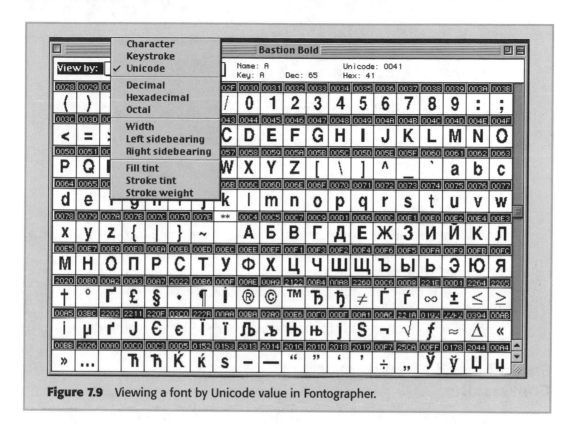

Figure 7.9 Viewing a font by Unicode value in Fontographer.

the characters overlap correctly. Figure 7.10 shows three renderings of the same Russian sentence. The first appears correctly. In the second, one character is amiss. In the third, a Unicode-compliant font, only a few of the characters appear correctly, even though most of them match their phonetic equivalents in the Latin alphabet.

If you are dealing with only a small number of documents that need to be converted in this way, and the differences are minor, it may simply be easiest to deal with them individually and make corrections by hand. For more complex conversions, you may need to use some of the methods discussed in the following sections.

Ghost Characters

Converting from fonts that don't exactly match each other (for example, from one Cyrillic font to another Cyrillic font with a slightly different mapping) may cause you to lose some characters. This happens

Мила мыло не любила, но мама мылом Милу мыла.

Мила мыла не лэбила, но мама мылом Милу мыла.

Mila myla ne l[bila, no mama mylom Milu myla.

Figure 7.10   The same Russian sentence rendered in three different fonts.

when positions that are occupied in one font are simply empty in another. You might then retype the missing characters and think that you have solved the problem, only to discover that strange symbols (boxes, for example) show up when you print. This is because the characters that you had "lost" are still there. They may not show up on screen, but they can still appear as null characters when you print. To fix this problem, try deleting on screen where the null characters appear on paper, even if there doesn't seem to be anything there.

Encoding and Character Set Conversions

An increasing number of applications, such as Web browsers, are able to handle encoding conversions automatically in order to render text properly. When this isn't possible and you have to convert data manually, there are two main options: algorithmic and table-driven conversions.

Algorithmic conversions. This option can be used when the characters in two different encodings are in the same order. You can apply a formula to convert the code points from one encoding to the code points for the next. Ken Lunde, manager of CJKV type development for Adobe Systems and author of *CJKV Information Processing*, says, "Algorithmic conversions can usually (but not always) be applied between encodings for the same locale, such as ISO-2022-JP, EUC-JP, and Shift-JIS for Japan."

Table-driven conversions. This option is used when characters in different encodings are not in the same order, or when there are different characters or different numbers of characters. It is relatively rare for two character encodings to have a one-to-one mapping. With this type of conversion, you must essentially say "this code point in this table equals this code point in this table."

"Table-driven conversion is required when dealing with Unicode and when converting across locales," says Lunde. The exception is when ASCII and ISO 8859-1:1998 are used. Unicode's support for Latin characters matches these encodings for the most common Western European characters.

Lunde says there are also some cases of code conversions within a single locale that require table-driven code conversion, such as half- to full-width katakana conversion for Japanese. Table-driven conversions may also be easiest when an algorithmic conversion is possible but especially complicated.

In addition to serving as a standard, Unicode can also be used as a table-driven information interchange code. To convert from one non-Unicode encoding to another, it may be easiest to convert one to Unicode and then convert from Unicode to the other encoding. Mapping tables may not already exist for a direct conversion from one non-Unicode encoding to another, but they may exist for converting these encodings to and from Unicode.

One example of how this is done is found in Java, which uses Unicode as its native character encoding but provides a set of classes that can convert many standard character encodings to and from Unicode. Java applications that deal with non-Unicode text usually convert the data to Unicode to process it, but then convert it back to an external character encoding. The two conversion classes for Java are ByteToChar, which converts from native, byte-oriented character sets to Unicode characters, and CharToByte, which converts from Unicode to byte-oriented character set encodings.

Details about character set conversion in Java are available from Sun Microsystems at http://java.sun.com/products/jdk/1.1/intl/html/intlspec.doc7.html, and a complete table of supported encodings is available at http://java.sun.com/products/jdk/1.1/docs/guide/intl/encoding.doc.html.

Exhaustive detail about these issues (primarily for CJKV issues, including code in Perl, C, and Java for conversions such as the ones mentioned here) is provided by Lunde in his book *CJKV Information Processing* (O'Reilly & Associates, 1999), and a sample Unicode-based CJKV converter written by Lunde in Perl is available from ftp://ftp.oreilly.com/pub/examples/nutshell/cjkv/perl/cjkvconv.pl.

One way that developers can quickly add support for conversions between Unicode and a broad range of widely used language-specific legacy encodings (end-user utilities are described in the following sections) is with *Rosette,* a C++ library for Unicode from Basis Technology (www.basistech.com/unicode). Usually embedded into applications and used to convert text from external sources into Unicode, Rosette can handle 22 character properties and 28 different scripts. It is portable across platforms including Windows, Macintosh, and common Unix variants, and can be licensed royalty-free.

Conversion Utilities

For smaller conversion jobs, you may be able to use the following conversion tools.

UConvert

The UConvert tool for Windows NT converts text files between the 16-bit Unicode character encoding and other traditional character encodings. It may also be used to install conversion tables, which are used by the Win32 API's MultiByteToWideChar and WideCharTo-MultiByte functions. UConvert can be downloaded from the page at http://msdn.microsoft.com/library/devprods/vs6/vc++/vcsample/vcsmpuconvert.htm.

To convert a file with UConvert to Unicode from an ANSI or other code page, open the File menu, click Open Source File, and specify the file you want to convert. In the Conversion menu, click Convert Now. Finally, in the File menu, click Save As and specify a name for the converted file.

You can use the Conversion menu to specify conversion options. For more information, see the help file UCONVERT.HLP, which is included with the Unicode Converter.

WinMass 2000

WinMASS 2000, from Star+Globe (www.starglobe.com), is a Windows utility that, in addition to enabling support for work in multilingual documents in English versions of Windows, has code-conversion features that make it possible for text files to be converted from one encoding scheme to another.

MacLinkPlus Deluxe

MacLinkPlus Deluxe, from DataViz (www.dataviz.com), is a Macintosh utility for converting files to and from Windows and other formats, and it also has the ability to handle some language encodings. As shown in Figure 7.11, by selecting a language in the Preferences window, it is possible to choose options for mapping extended ASCII

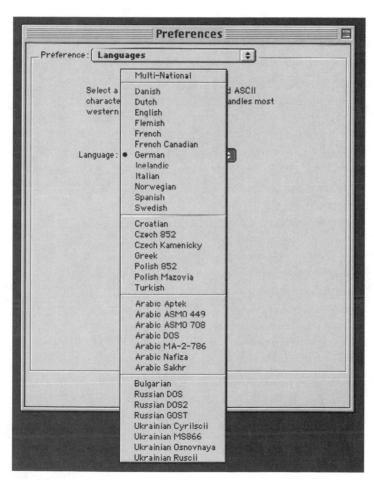

Figure 7.11 MacLinkPlus Deluxe can handle character-encoding conversions.

characters to or from various other encodings during the file-format conversion of word-processing, spreadsheet, and database files. The MultiNational default setting accommodates most of the languages that originated in Western Europe.

Next

Parts One and Two of this book look at setting up basic multilingual support, as well as the development and creation of multilingual applications and other resources. The next and final section of the book, Part Three, looks at multilingual communications and content.

Multilingual Communications and Content

Translation and Localization

As part of the overall process of internationalization, translation and localization require particular attention. This chapter looks at some of the issues involved in preparing applications and related materials for different locales worldwide, as well as an overview of tools for translators, options for *automatic* translation, and tools for localization. This chapter also provides advice on how to choose a localization service if you decide to outsource and how to write documentation and Website content that is both understandable to a broad international readership and more easily translatable.

Major Issues in Translation and Localization

Understandably, software developers may be most concerned about whether an application works correctly. It might seem that if it does what it is supposed to and doesn't crash, then they've done their job. For a global market, unfortunately, this focus on functionality is necessary but not sufficient.

A product may work well technically, and even be a commercial success in a particular locale—the United States, for example—but preparing it for the rest of the world isn't easy. Inadequate preparation for localization during development can result in delays, budget over-runs, or even product recalls as a result of errors. A localized version of a product that takes too long to come out may lose market share. Products that have been poorly localized, or that have poorly trans-lated documentation or sales and promotional material, may sell poorly and can even be an embarrassment to the sales staff in the country where they are intended to be marketed.

Major issues to keep in mind when laying the groundwork for suc-cessful internationalization are discussed in Chapter 5, "Strategies for Multilingual Development and Internationalization." But there are also a number of issues to keep in mind when you get to the point of localization—that is, carrying out your internationalization plans and actually creating the localized versions of your applications. Localiza-tion is one way that internationalization is put into practice, and the issues involved are examined here.

Use Quality Translation Services

Because translation services vary so widely in their experience, exper-tise, and the languages they cover, it is difficult to make general rec-ommendations about what to look for in terms of price. As a rule of thumb, however, it makes sense to pay more to get better-quality ser-vice. If a poor translation means that extensive changes will have to be made, or, worse, that a product is unsuccessful, using a qualified ser-vice can pay for itself many times over.

Look closely at translators' specializations. Expertise in technical com-munication and the language you need may not be enough. A transla-tor who has done excellent translations of documentation for enterprise-level server software may be less qualified when it comes to translations about desktop publishing and the terminology that is unique to this or most any other field. It can be difficult—or maybe impossible—for translators to translate what they do not fully under-stand even in the source language. Make sure that your translators are qualified to handle the specifics of the projects that you undertake.

Do Not Rely on Native Speakers within Your Organization

Although it can be helpful to have native speakers of other languages who already work within your organization take a look at completed

Unique and Sufficient?

Occasionally you'll encounter documents that have obviously been written or translated by people who are not completely fluent in English. The results may sound like these real examples:

"Company X is offering various significant products in categories like Spread-Sheet, Graphic Tools, Database, Groupware."

"Company Y is an Internet provider highly recognized for its unique and sufficient number of multimedia contents."

While both of these sentences are basically understandable, you probably don't want your company to sound like this in another language. Don't settle for "unique and sufficient" in your translations. Use qualified translators and ask native speakers who are familiar with the field you work in to check these translations.

translations and evaluate the work done by professional translators, it is generally not a good idea to make them responsible for translating. Translation is a skill that includes but goes beyond a knowledge of two or more languages. In addition, members of your organization who speak other languages presumably have other responsibilities. They may not be able to meet these responsibilities or do translations well if they are asked to do both.

Testing

In addition to the usual functionality testing that has to be done with any software, localized applications must also be tested for the language they use in the user interface, dialog boxes, and error messages; their ability to display and print non-Latin text; locale-specific formatting of dates, time, numbers and other data; and their help systems, input methods, and fallback locales (which ensure that if a locale-specific file is missing, the application does not, for example, crash or fail to provide a message). Test results and information on unresolved problems may also need to be shared with customer support—perhaps in several countries, if you have offices abroad.

If you do in-house quality-assurance testing, all of these issues will need to be addressed, or you may want to seek help from a localization services company that can handle both functional and locale-specific testing so that you can concentrate on the main-language version of your product. It is also a good idea to test localized applications on all localized variants of the operating systems they run under.

For a detailed checklist of internationalization testing issues, see the pages maintained by the Sun Developer's Connection at http://soldc.sun.com/developer/articles/i18n/index.html. Free access is available by registering for a login name and password.

NOTE   The Language Technology Resource Center, a division of MultiLingual Computing, Inc. (www.multilingual.com), the publisher of *MultiLingual Computing & Technology* magazine, maintains a multilingual testing lab for Unix, Windows 9x and NT, OS/2, and Macintosh applications.

Corrections and Fixes

Making sure that known bugs and other problems (such as incorrect or inappropriate translations) are fixed requires good organization even if you're only dealing with one version of a product. When that product is localized, new allowances need to be made.

If you use a database to keep track of known or suspected bugs, you may need to modify it to take into account the different localized versions of your products. Specify whether a particular problem affects all versions of the product, only the localized versions (in other words, not the primary version), or just some of the individual localized versions.

Depending on the answers to these questions, who will be responsible for making sure that these problems are fixed, and that they don't remain unfixed because the necessary cooperation isn't happening? For example, if the people who wrote the code that is involved in a particular problem don't speak the language that the problem appears in, they may need help from localization to fix it. It can be helpful to have someone coordinate this and to make sure that your procedures for fixing the bugs in your software realistically reflect the international complexity of these products.

NOTE

For many of these issues, you may also wish to seek help from one of the many companies that specialize in localization and translation services and have specific experience in dealing with the problems that can arise with localized products. Information and advice about how to select a localization services company is included later in this chapter.

An online listing of hundreds of translation agencies is available at www.hake .com/translators/index.html-ssi, or you may also wish to consult *Glenn's Guide to Translation Agencies* (John M. Glenn, 1999). For more information, see www .glennsguide.com.

Support Programming

Wes Nakamura, a software localizer, emphasizes that localization programming doesn't only involve direct work with the source code itself (to enable double-byte support, for example). You may also need to plan for *support programming*.

"This can involve all sorts of custom text and file handling, often unique to the project and depending on the needs of the moment," Nakamura says. "I often write programs that deal with text files, replacing strings, examining resource files, or attempting to reuse as much of a previous translation as possible." Support programming such as this makes it easier for translators to concentrate on translation, not technical issues.

Changes and Cutoff Dates

Cutoff dates for changes to applications, documentation, Web pages, and other related materials need to be especially clear for internationalized products. The addition of a feature—or even the change of a single word—may have to be implemented in all the different localized versions of an application and its related materials. The list of people whose work may be affected by changes includes developers, marketers, salespeople, trainers, technical writers, graphic designers, product managers, customer support staff, testers, and translators. The impact of changes is multiplied by the number of languages or locales you are dealing with, and even if there are only one or two people in each of these areas who need to be informed of last-minute changes, keeping in touch with them all can be daunting.

To meet deadlines despite this interdependence, it is important for everyone to understand the stakes involved when dealing with a product that is being localized. Someone may need to ensure that materials are ready to be passed on to avoid unnecessary revisions and changes, to monitor and schedule the changes that may take place, and to determine when it is no longer possible to make changes without delaying the project.

Naturally, even with the best-laid plans there will probably be some unexpected surprises. If possible, it can be a good idea to plan for more time than you think a localization project will take, and to make sure that staff and resources are available for last-minute work that can't be avoided. In the words of Michael Cárdenas, president of Multilingual Translations, "No matter how prepared you think you are, prepare some more." Localization is one case in which if something can go wrong, it will, and the problems can be particularly cumbersome to deal with.

Review and Communication

To make sure that your offices, subsidiaries, or distributors worldwide can successfully market, sell, and support your localized product, it is important to include these people in the review process for the localized product as it moves toward release. This can help to ensure that the most appropriate wording and style is used, and can help to avoid last-minute surprises that cause delays or hamper the successful marketing or sales of a product.

To do this it may help to establish a formal review process in which distributors and others who will be responsible for localized products are given translations to review and comment on in a timely manner. Their comments will also need to be returned in time to be evaluated and, as necessary, incorporated without holding up the rest of the project.

Depending on your organization, it may not be enough to simply send out translations and hope that your reviewers will look at them and get back to you in time with comments or concerns. All this coordination is complicated enough that it may make sense to give someone the specific responsibility for making sure that review and communication about the translations in your localized products happen in step with the rest of your project's timetable.

This process of review and communication may also be complicated if the reviewers are scattered in different locations around the world.

The OpenTag Initiative

The OpenTag Initiative is a working group in which both localization services and clients can participate in defining a new standard that supports open data-encoding methods during the localization process. The OpenTag markup format makes translation assets such as translation-memory databases independent of the tools used to create them, making them easier to exchange and reuse.

For more information about the OpenTag Initiative, see www.opentag.org.

When live discussions would be helpful, it may make sense to use video or conference calls and to schedule them around time-zone differences as necessary.

Tools for Translators

This section describes a variety of tools that are available to make translation easier.

One of the most important of these tools is *translation-memory technology*. Translation-memory tools simplify translation by compiling a database of the source and target-language text from previous translations. Then, while you are working on a new translation, it compares the new source text to the database. When it finds a match or a similarity, it suggests a translation based on the translation work that has already been done. The translator has the option of either accepting this translation with a mouse click, or making changes as necessary. Figure 8.1 shows the popular tool *Translator's Workbench* (described in more detail later). The sentence in the uppermost window closely matches a sentence that has been found in the translation-memory database, and in Microsoft Word, the suggested translation has been added pending editing or approval.

The advantage of using translation-memory technology is not only that it makes translation work easier and faster, it also helps to ensure greater consistency. The same instructions (such as "To create an object . . .") might be translated in a number of different ways into a target language, but translation-memory technology helps to ensure that the same translations are used, even if different translators are working on the same project—which can avoid unnecessary confusion. Translation-memory technology might not do you much good

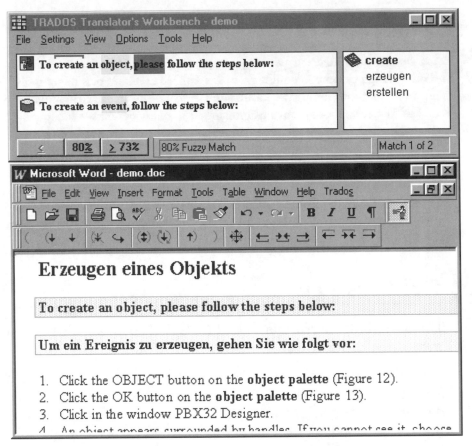

Figure 8.1 Using the translation-memory tool Translator's Workbench.

for translating literature or other texts that contain more original language, but it works especially well for software manuals, which can contain variations on the same simple instructions over and over again in different contexts.

The following are some translation tools available today. Freely downloadable evaluation copies of many of the tools are available through the designated Web sites.

Déjà Vu

Déjà Vu, from Language Partners International (www.languagepartners .com/dvi), is a translation-memory tool for Windows 95/98 and NT. Déjà Vu includes TermWatch, an integrated terminology-management system, and the File Alignment Wizard, which allows you to create memory databases from translations you have done in the past. Déjà Vu can also import and export translation databases in the format of TRA-DOS Translator's Workbench, and supports the use of the OpenTag format for easier exchange of translation-memory databases.

LANTSCAPE

LANTSCAPE, from LANT (www.lant.com), is a product for managing translation requests on an intranet. Users who need to have a document translated submit it as an HTML, ASCII, or RTF file through a secure intranet connection. They then specify the kind of translation they need. If they need only a rough, automatic translation, LANTSCAPE runs the job through the integrated LANTMARK automatic translation system. If they need a professional translation, LANTSCAPE sends the text to a designated translator either within or outside of your organization.

TranslationManager

TranslationManager, from IBM (www.qsoft.de/ibmtrans/ibmtrans .htm), is a machine-assisted translation tool for professional translators. It runs under Windows 3.1 and higher, as well as OS/2. TranslationManager includes a translation editor for original text, localization support for translating text in program code, dictionary-management tools for specialized dictionaries, translation-memory tools, and the ability to exchange project-specific translation-memory databases. TranslationManager supports common text and publishing formats and provides support for a variety of European source languages, as well as Japanese. It can be used for translation into any language supported by the translator's operating system.

TransLexis (www.qsoft.de/ibmtrans/translex.htm) is a related tool for companywide terminology management, based on a relational database and including components for exporting and importing lexical and terminological data.

Translator's Workbench and Other TRADOS Tools

One of the most widely used translation-memory products, Translator's Workbench, from TRADOS (www.trados.com), runs under Windows 95/98 or NT. It can be directly accessed from a word processor and is especially closely integrated with Microsoft Word. As you translate, Workbench memorizes your work and offers suggestions based on previous translations of identical or similar phrases and sentences. When matches are not exact, Workbench expresses the extent to which you have a match (as a percentage) and offers options as necessary to complete the translation.

Other translation tools available from TRADOS for use with Translator's Workbench include *WinAlign*, which can build translation-memory databases from existing translations; *MultiTerm*, which can store an unlimited number of terms in up to 20 languages; and *MultiTerm Dictionary*, which lets you compile and distribute online dictionaries (which can be combined with existing dictionaries).

Another TRADOS tool is the *S-Tagger*, a Windows application that provides an interface between translation-memory or machine-translation systems and FrameMaker or InterLeaf files (used for building and publishing books).

WebBudget

Aquino Software's WebBudget (www.webbudget.com) is a budgeting and billing tool for translators of Web pages and Web-site owners who are interested in localizing their sites. Available for Windows 95/98 and NT, WebBudget locates, classifies, and counts translatable text in Internet files (from folders and subfolders on disk or online), including META tags, Java messages, and ALT words, to give a better idea of the true size of a Web translation project.

Workbench

Workbench, from SDL International (www.sdlint.com), works with the company's translation database tool, sdlx. It remembers a user's translations and automatically offers other possible translations and terminology from the user's translation database within Microsoft Word. Workbench can also work with other file formats, such as RTF files.

Automatic or Machine Translation

Automatic or machine translation is a controversial topic. There is no doubt that computer technology can assist human translators, and it can even produce translations that are quite understandable. However, there

Resources from the American Translators Association

The American Translators Association (ATA) makes several publications available, including the booklet *A Consumer's Guide to Good Translation* and the *ATA Translation Services Directory*, which indexes active ATA members by language, subject, and state or country. The ATA also holds an annual conference each November, which includes exhibits and workshops on language technology. For more information, visit the ATA site at www.atanet.org.

is reason to doubt whether computers will ever be able to perform completely reliable translations until (and if) they are able to use language and understand the world in the same way that human beings do.

Part of the reason for this is that there is no perfect one-to-one correspondence between the words in one language and the words in another, and even technical writing can be surprisingly idiomatic (see the *Writing Globally* section later in this chapter). Attempts to accommodate every nuance of meaning with automatic translation software may be an ultimately futile attempt that can only ever approach—but never meet—the quality that can be achieved by qualified human translators. Professional translators are still required for important translation work.

Ironically, even the text on the Web sites for some of the translation products described in this chapter appear to have been translated into English that is understandable, but still a little awkward. The site for one well-known corporation's translation products uses phrases such as "consists on" and "It does not only help you tackle the vast amount of translation needs efficiently. . . ." It's impossible to say whether this understandable but awkward phrasing is the result of machine translation or human error, but in either case it demonstrates the importance of double-checking the text that appears on your Web site and other publications.

Tools such as this can also be used to produce a draft translation to start from, but the industry preference leans toward translation-memory tools that compile a database of previously translated sentences and phrases and suggest matches when something similar is encountered. Translation-memory tools make translating easier and less repetitive, while still ensuring that there is human oversight of the entire translation.

The upshot of this is that there is no magic solution—no way to get cheap, fast, perfect translations from a machine. Having said this, however, an imperfect translation is usually better than no translation at all. Except in cases where a crucial word or two cannot be translated, the results of machine translation are usually quite understandable, if a little awkward. Convoluted wording and confusing word choice can make it difficult to read more than a few pages of machine-translated texts, but automatic translation tools like the ones from the companies briefly described here can do a good job of making short texts from other languages accessible.

Babylon Single Click Translator (www.babylon.com). A free software utility that makes it possible for Windows users to translate English words and expressions into Spanish, German, French, Italian, Dutch, Japanese, and Hebrew. A version is available for each of these languages. The utility uses on-screen optical character recognition (OCR) to recognize text anywhere on the computer screen that the user clicks.

Enterprise Translation Server (www.transparent.com). This product, from Transparent Language, offers the ability to do automatic translations in network, intranet, and Internet environments. Translations can be performed from English to Spanish, French, German, Italian, and Portuguese, and from Spanish, French, and German into English.

LANTMARK (www.lant.com/lantmark.htm). This product is an automatic enterprise-level translation system designed for high-volume translation needs in industry and government. LANTMARK is not available as an off-the-shelf product, but rather is customized to an organization's needs.

Lernout & Hauspie (www.lhsl.com). Makes several machine-translation products (some of which were formerly distributed under the name Globalink), including *Power Translator Pro*, which translates documents and Web pages to and from English, Spanish, German, French, Italian, and Portuguese, and a family of *iTranslator* products, which provide translation solutions for Internet and organizational environments. iTranslator languages include the major Western European languages and Arabic, Chinese, Japanese, and Korean.

SYSTRAN (www.systransoft.com). Makes a variety of automatic translation products for Windows users, ranging from personal translation software to enterprise-level translation systems for intranets, extranets, and LANs, all in a variety of language pairs. SYSTRAN's business product, *SYSTRAN Professional,* offers the ability to create user-defined dictionaries and includes 21 industry-specific glossaries for context-sensitive translations. *SYSTRAN PRO* is available in 14 language pairs and can be used from within the Microsoft Word toolbar; it supports RTF, ASCII, ANSI, HTML, and SGML files.

SYSTRAN also provides the translation technology for AltaVista's *Babelfish* (http://babelfish.altavista.com) translation site, which offers translations to and from English and five other languages: French, German, Italian, Portuguese, and Spanish. The site allows you to enter text to be translated or to enter the URL for a Web page, which is then displayed in your browser after all of the page's text has been translated.

Translation Experts (www.tranexp.com). Makes a family of automatic translation products including *Word Translator,* a multilingual dictionary, and *InterTran,* which can translate documents between dozens of language pairs. InterTran is available on the Web at www.tranexp .com/InterTran.cgi, or as a desktop product for Windows and Macintosh. A high-end product called *Neural Translator,* based on neural-network technology, is available, as well.

Tools for Localization

A number of tools are designed specifically for localization. They help to carry out, manage, and test the changes that need to be made to an application to bring it to local markets around the world. The following are examples of some of the main types of localization products that are available.

Catalyst (www.corel.ie/catalyst). Catalyst, from Corel, offers an integrated localization environment for Windows 95/98 and NT applications. Catalyst makes it possible to combine all files (DLLs, EXEs, INIs, and so forth) into a single file called a *Translation Toolkit* for easier project management during the localization process. Other features include a suite of editors for user-interface and help-system translation, quality-assurance tools, and the Leverage Expert, which allows translations from previous versions of a product to be used.

There are also language assistants, which help ensure consistency between terms used in the user-interface and help documentation, and an extensible application programming interface for working with custom resources.

Localization Guru (www.beta-sigma.com). This tool, from Beta-Sigma Data Systems, is for VisualBasic developers who want to create multilingual user-interface applications, and it is licensed royalty-free. The developer creates the primary-language version of the application and uses Localization Guru to export text from the application to a language database. This extracted text can then be translated by human translators into one or more languages and added to the application so that the user-interface language can be set by the user.

Multilizer (www.multilizer.com). A localization tool with editions designed for use with Visual J++, Delphi, C++Builder, JBuilder, and VisualBasic. Multilizer allows development and maintenance to take place in English versions of Windows, for example, and allows translation to take place with the application's Language Manager utility on different platforms, making it possible to leverage earlier translations into new versions and to add new languages without programming or recompiling.

rcTest (www.rubric.com). This testing tool, from Rubric, Inc., is meant to improve localization quality assurance by standardizing testing procedures. The tool's recording, tracking, and reporting capabilities can be used to manage testing procedures across platforms, screen resolutions, and user options.

Superlinguist (www.ktintl.com). This family of localization tools, from KT International, includes *Superlinguist Manager,* which is designed for the localization of user interfaces without source-code changes, *Superlinguist Resources Manager,* which simplifies resource file translation and version control, and *Superlinguist Resource Editor,* which simplifies the resizing of dialog boxes for translated words and phrases.

TurboSFX (www.pgcc.com). This wizard system, from Pacific Gold Coast, for creating self-extracting archive files allows messages and scripts in Windows-supported languages.

VisualBasic Language Manager Pro (www.whippleware.com). This product, from WhippleWare, is designed to help manage the localization of VisualBasic applications. VBLM makes it possible to maintain a single unmodified copy of source code while building local-ized versions for any number of languages. VBLM runs under all versions of Windows, works with all versions of VisualBasic except version 1, and requires no royalties or runtime fees.

Working with a Localization Services Company

It may be that you can't or don't want to deal with localization inter-nally. You may lack the time, the resources, the linguistic expertise, or simply the inclination to set up everything that would be necessary to do all of your own localization, or you might want to go with an out-side company that has more experience.

If you do decide to work with an outside localization services com-pany, Bert Esselink, author of *A Practical Guide to Software Localization: For Translators, Engineers and Project Managers* (John Benjamins, 1998) recommends looking at a number of criteria in selecting a company, such as experience with similar localization projects, staff and resource availability, quality procedures, and financial stability.

Level of Outsourcing

It is important to think about how you want to work with a localiza-tion services company, because this will determine the kind of com-pany you should choose.

"Companies need to decide on the level of outsourcing they want for their projects and products," Esselink says. "If they want to outsource all project management, engineering, DTP, and possibly even testing to a localization vendor, the best option is to have an MLV—a multi-language vendor—handle several languages and services." A com-pany such as this may be best suited to take over all or most aspects of a localization project. "Most software companies choose to work with a selection of 'major players', like multilanguage vendors that central-ize project management and technical services," Esselink says.

On the other hand, you might want more in-house control or oversight over the localization process on a daily basis, or you might want to spread any risks by not giving responsibility for an entire localization effort to one company. If this is the approach you prefer, a better choice may be to work with several single-language vendors who can all concentrate on one language.

In either case, it's a good idea to plan on having more of a relationship with the localization services company that you choose, rather than simply handing off a project that you can't or would rather not do in-house.

"The 'we're paying you to do this' type of attitude is not as common as it was before," says Christopher Hanaoka, director of worldwide research and development for Bowne Global Solutions. Hanaoka says he has seen an evolution in the localization industry toward working relationships that benefit localization services companies and their clients. "Seven years ago it was very much a customer-vendor relationship. After releasing the U.S. versions of their products, our customers would say, 'I'm burned out, you do it.' Now we're sort of moving up the product life cycle. They're actually talking to us before they finish coding. People like the Microsofts and the Novells and the Corels have become much more involved. It's much more of a relationship." The result of this cooperation is that projects go more smoothly with fewer potentially costly and time-consuming changes or corrections along the way.

An excellent source of information about choosing and working with a translation agency is the detailed white paper "3 Steps to Successful Translation Management: How to Minimize Costs and Maximize Quality," from ForeignExchange Translations. The paper offers dozens of specific suggestions, such as testing a translation service by asking them to do a small, paid project first, asking about who and how many people will be working on your translation project, and getting a dedicated contact person at the agency you work with who will be familiar with the day-to-day progress being made on your project. This white paper is available from the ForeignExchange site at www.fxtrans.com/faq.htm. ForeignExchange also distributes a free email newsletter, *Multilingual Compliance News,* on language, technology, and regulations that affect the industry.

Security

Outsourcing your localization means that you may be transferring unreleased code and other potentially valuable information outside the company. It is a good idea to ask about security procedures and potential conflicts of interest, such as having one of your competitors as a client. It's not unusual for the same localization services company to be working on projects for competing companies, but if this is the case, it's important to make sure that appropriate security measures are taken.

Finding a Localization Services Company

Good sources for information about localization service companies are the articles, advertisements, and listings in the bimonthly magazine *MultiLingual Computing & Technology* (www.multilingual.com). At the back of each issue is an extensive buyer's guide which lists services that specialize in localization, translation, and other areas.

Another source of information about the localization industry itself and industry practices is the Localisation Industry Standards Association (LISA). LISA's site (www.lisa.unige.ch) offers information about the association's workshops, meetings, publications, and special-interest groups.

Finally, the Localization Institute (www.localization-institute.org) provides seminars, training, conferences, and other resources about topics such as localization project management and localization tools and technologies. The institute is not affiliated with any localization service or tool provider.

Writing Globally

An important aspect of developing an application for the global market is the documentation that is written to explain it. Ideally, documentation should be written with a broadly international audience in mind: native readers of the primary language the documentation is written in, nonnative readers of the primary language, and translators who must translate the text into other languages.

The same is true for Web content, which may need to be translated, and which may be accessed from anywhere in the world by people whose ability to read in one or another language may be limited.

Dovie Wylie, who holds a doctorate in linguistics and is president of On-Site English (www.on-site-english.com), is a consultant and trainer who specializes in teaching how to write for an international audience.

The key, she says, is clarity and a lack of ambiguity. Both of these qualities in writing will help nonnative readers and translators alike.

NOTE

The assumption in this section is that your writing is being done in English first, although many of these principles apply generally to writing in other languages as well.

One way to make your writing more clear, Wylie says, is to avoid confusing idioms wherever possible.

"You would think that technical writing doesn't contain any idioms, but it does all the time. It doesn't take much imagination to see that something like 'the world is your oyster' is going to cause problems, but something like 'as it turns out' or 'turn up' can too," she says. "We use these phrasal verbs very easily, and a lot of them can be replaced."

To appreciate the confusion this can cause for nonnative readers, Wylie suggests opening a dictionary and looking up a word like *turn* or *run* to see how many phrasal verbs you can find, such as *run across, run down, run into*, and so forth. Each of these combinations has its own meaning—only a few of which may involve any actual running, turning, and so forth—and can be hard for nonnative readers to understand. It is impossible to remove all idioms from writing, but it can help to avoid the ones that may be obvious sources of confusion.

Another tip is to avoid needless modal auxiliaries, such as *could, may,* and *should,* which can cause confusion. The word *should,* for example, can mean that something is advisable, as in "You should make a backup copy of this file," or that something is a reasonable assumption, as in "You should be ready to run the application now." You can rewrite these sentences as "Make a backup copy of this file" and "If you completed the installation successfully, run the application," respectively.

Other advice is not to take the deletions that English allows. In the sentence "If I have a headache, then I take aspirin," the word *then* can be deleted, but Wylie says it's best to leave these in. "I have had nonnative speakers say, 'We like to see those words in there because they signal to us what's coming.'" Another tip is to avoid needless negative constructions. "'He won't be here until March' is hard for readers to get through," Wylie says. "'He's coming in March' is simpler."

One way to train yourself to write this way is to think about the level of formality you are trying to convey. Wylie points out that English lacks some ways to signal formality in speech, such as the distinction between *tú* and *Usted* in Spanish (both mean "you," but *tú* is informal and is used with friends and close relatives, while *Usted* is used with people you don't know well, or as a sign of respect). As a result, English speakers tend to use some of the grammatical constructions described here to convey informality. Using a phrasal verb in the sentence "They called off the meeting" sounds a little more conversational than "They canceled the meeting." Unfortunately, this tendency toward informality can make technical and business writing less clear to nonnative readers and translators.

Wylie offers training in these methods in a one-day workshop and says that in the long run, it's usually better for an organization to train its own writers than to send work out. "This is not that hard, and it's not like it takes a long time to learn," she says. She also says that writing with an international audience in mind can be done in a way that is clear for everyone, without sounding stilted. "When this is done well, native readers won't notice anything strange," she says. "We don't want to end up with a writing style that ends up sounding like a first-grade reader."

Wylie adds that translators also appreciate this style of writing because it eliminates ambiguity. "Writing globally is writing out of the core of English. The varieties of English spoken around the world have a common core. Write from that."

Wylie offers an article with additional tips about global writing, which is available by contacting her at dovie@on-site-english.com.

Global Writing Sources

Coe, Marlana. *Human Factors for Technical Communicators* (John Wiley & Sons, 1996).

Controlled Languages (www-uilots.let.ruu.nl/Controlled-languages) provides information about a variety of tools available to help write simplified or *controlled* English.

Haramundanis, Katherine. *The Art of Technical Documentation* (Digital Equipment Corporation, 1992).

Hoft, Nancy L. *International Technical Communication: How to Export Information About High Technology* (John Wiley & Sons, 1995).

Mulhaus-Moyer, Ursula. "Improving Translation Consistency." *Multi-Lingual Computing & Technology* 9(6):36–37.

Nancy Hoft Consulting (www.world-ready.com/r_intl.htm) offers links to resources on global English and an extensive bibliography.

Payne, Daniel S. "A Checklist for Preparing Global Documentation." *MultiLingual Computing & Technology* 10(1):47–48.

Paper versus Electronic Documents

If your documentation contains non-Latin text, you may want to consider electronic distribution through a cross-platform format such as portable document format (PDF) instead of in print. PDF documents with non-Latin text don't require the reader to have the same fonts or language support used to create them. Neither does paper, of course, but by distributing electronically instead of on paper you save yourself the expense of printing multiple language versions of the same document and the trouble of working with non-Latin scripts in print.

If paper is the best way to distribute your documents, however, details about multilingual publishing options are offered in Chapter 10, "Multilingual Publishing, Graphic Design, and Multimedia."

For More Information

See the Institute of Electrical and Electronics Engineers' (IEEE's) *Guide to Translation and Localization: Preparing Products for Foreign Markets* (IEEE Computer Society Press, 1999). This 96-page guide discusses the preparation of documentation, software, and Web sites for the global market.

A series of handbooks on the localization of software, HTML, and documentation is available to interested companies from the localization company Rubric at www.rubric.com/local/handbooks.html.

Next

The next chapter looks at another aspect of multilingual communication and content: email and other interactivity with non-Latin text.

CHAPTER 9

Multilingual Electronic Communication

Multilingual electronic communication is still somewhat difficult. Although support for a variety of standard character sets—sometimes including the universal character set Unicode—is available, you generally can't yet assume that all the potential recipients of an email message created with non-ASCII text, for example, will be able to correctly receive and read the content.

This chapter discusses the options for making multilingual electronic communication easier, with a focus on email and multilingual email applications, as well as newsreaders, the use of interactive Web forms with non-Latin text, and multilingual personal digital assistants.

Email

Before looking at individual email applications and their multilingual abilities, it can be helpful to review some of the major issues that affect multilingual email.

Earlier in the history of the Internet, electronic mail was limited to messages coded with 7-bit ASCII text and sent through Simple Mail

Transfer Protocol (SMTP) which didn't itself support the use of any other characters. Today, thanks to Multipurpose Internet Mail Extensions (MIME) encodings, which describe what sort of data is in a message and how it is encoded, this limit can be overcome, but problems still arise.

One of these problems is that older mail-server software may drop the eighth bit in transit, which makes messages in Western European languages with diacritic marks confusing or incomprehensible. Figure 9.1 shows the characters of the ISO Latin 1 set as seen in the Windows Character Map utility, which displays characters in rows of 32 characters. There is essentially one row for each bit, but the first 32 characters are not shown because they are reserved for internal commands and nonprinting formatting characters (start of text, carriage return, and so forth). The bottom row shows the characters that are represented by the eighth bit. The characters in this row are the characters that are lost if the eighth bit is dropped.

Even when the eighth bit and the characters it is used to represent are processed correctly, however, truly multilingual email requires many more than just 256 characters to handle all the world's writing systems.

For some languages it is possible to work within a 256-character limit by replacing the "upper rows" of a font with characters from another

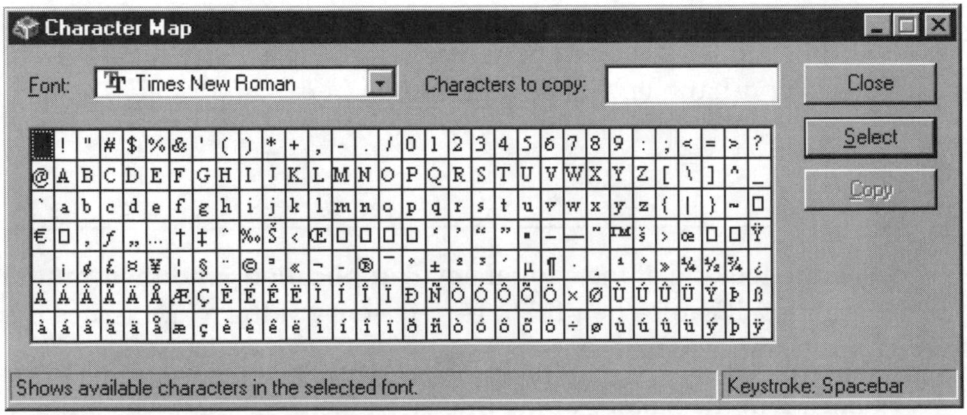

Figure 9.1 The characters of the ISO Latin 1 set.

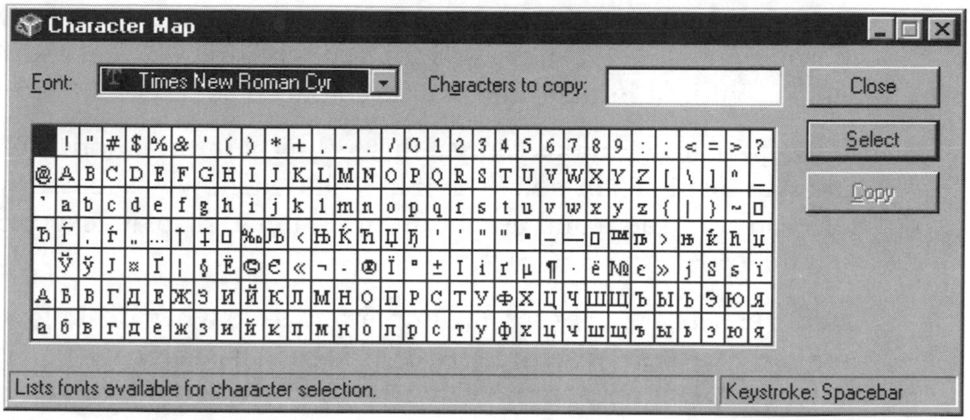

Figure 9.2   The Cyrillic version of the font Times New Roman.

alphabet, such as Greek or Cyrillic. Figure 9.1 shows the characters available in the Western version of the font Times New Roman. Figure 9.2 shows the Cyrillic version of Times New Roman (Latin characters for non-English languages have been replaced with Cyrillic characters), and Figure 9.3 shows the Greek version (Latin characters for non-English languages have been replaced with Greek characters).

Messages written in fonts such as these can be successfully sent and received through email as long as the software supports MIME, both sender and recipient are using the same character set, and the recipient has the same or an equivalent font.

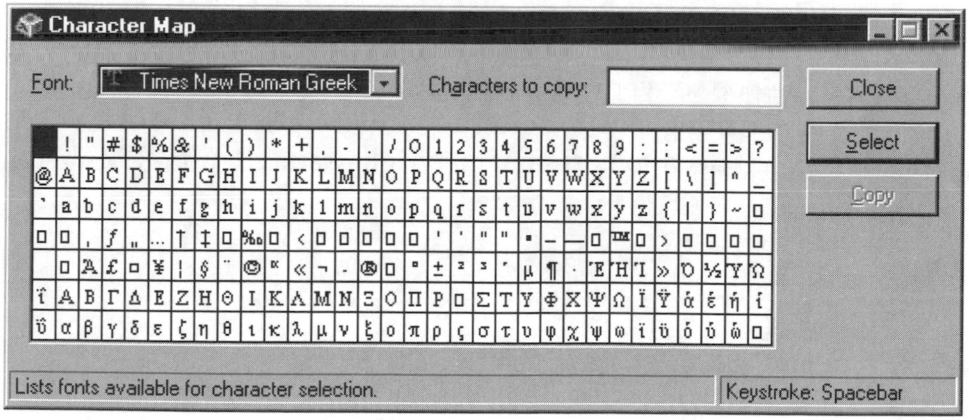

Figure 9.3   The Greek version of the font Times New Roman.

Figure 9.4 shows the header for an email message that contains MIME information about the message's content type (in this case, text that is *plain*, or without formatting) and the character set used.

Many email applications conceal this technical information or offer the option to display it or not. Even if it is hidden, however, email applications can still read it and use this information to display text correctly with the proper character set.

Character sets are an especially important issue when dealing with non-Latin scripts. Western European languages nearly always use the extended ASCII/ISO Latin 1 character set today, but for other scripts there can be more than one character set still in common use, such as the KOI8 and ISO Cyrillic character sets for Cyrillic-alphabet languages, or JIS, Shift-JIS, and EUC for Japanese.

To send email using character sets such as these, it is necessary for both sender and recipient to be using the same character set (or at least to have the ability to switch or convert as needed) and a font that can correctly display this character set. Even if a message is received using the proper character set, it won't be possible to display the message correctly without a font that includes the correct characters and glyphs.

There are several ways to work around these requirements if they present a problem for you or your recipients.

If your recipient uses the same word-processing application, platform, and fonts that you do, you can send your messages as attachments. If your recipient doesn't have the same application, it may help to save your document as plain text (or HTML) before sending it. This will make it possible for most other applications to open it, and it can then be converted back to the intended language if the recipient has a matching font. If necessary, you can also send copies of fonts, but you'll need to keep font copyright issues in mind. Some fonts

```
MIME-Version: 1.0
Content-Type: text/plain; charset=iso-8859-5
Content-Transfer-Encoding: 8bit
```

Figure 9.4 Email messages are sent with information about their content and character set.

may be licensed only for use on one computer, or at one location, and sending large fonts for Asian languages can also be cumbersome.

Other possibilities include exchanging multilingual messages as Adobe Acrobat files, or creating a graphic image of your message and sending it in formats such as GIF or JPEG. These methods are somewhat inconvenient, but they can work.

Fortunately, a growing number of email applications can handle a variety of character sets, allow the sender of a message to choose a character set in which to create a message, and can correctly identify the character sets of the messages they receive. The capabilities of these applications are examined in this chapter.

What About Unicode?

After all the emphasis placed on the universal character set Unicode in previous chapters, you might be wondering why this chapter has not yet presented any significant discussion of Unicode as a solution to the problems that arise with multilingual email.

The Unicode character set *does* provide a solution for these difficulties, but the ability to correctly handle Unicode by email is still limited at this time. Mail servers generally will not have a problem with Unicode, but as Farid Harmoush of Alis Technologies (maker of Tango Mail, described later in this chapter), says, "Receiving clients are another story."

"Support for Unicode is increasing, but it is still limited and uneven," Harmoush says. "Support for the UTF-8 encoding is beginning to be widespread, but often the user must configure the application and provide a Unicode font or install language packs."

In other words, Unicode is just one of the character sets that a good multilingual email application should be able to deal with. As Unicode gains wider acceptance, it may displace other character sets and become a kind of global email standard, but this hasn't happened yet.

If you and your email correspondents are all able to use Unicode, then it makes sense to use it. But at this stage, it is still likely that you will need to configure your email application for use with other character sets as described in the following section.

Brevity and International Netiquette

Over the last several years in the "developed world," we have generally gotten used to having unlimited (or at least inexpensive) access to email. Unfortunately, free or inexpensive Internet access isn't a reality everywhere yet, and some users are still using slow connections and may pay by the kilobyte (or the minute) for the email they receive. This makes it important to avoid sending long messages (especially if they are unsolicited) or large attachments if you are unsure whether you might be inadvertently clogging up your recipient's access to the Internet or running up their bill.

In a case like this, if you need to send a long message or large attachment, it is courteous to ask whether the recipient really wants it. You aren't likely to run into this problem with email correspondents in major cities, but it can still be an issue for recipients in smaller cities, less developed countries, and remote areas.

Email Applications

Previously limited mostly to U.S.-ASCII text, email applications are becoming more sophisticated in their ability to deal with non-Latin and multilingual texts. This section profiles some of the leaders. As it is impossible in many cases to give detailed instructions for all language versions, Web links to further details are provided.

Netscape Communicator

The built-in email functions in Netscape Communicator (www .netscape.com) share the multilingual capabilities of the Navigator Web browser.

If the character set for an incoming message cannot be identified automatically, Communicator gives you the ability to try different character sets manually. To do this, pull down the View menu and go to the Character Set submenu, shown in Figure 9.5. This submenu gives options for character sets that cover most of the world's script systems.

In order to receive messages that use different character sets, you may also need to choose a font to use with a particular character set.

To do this, pull down the Edit menu and go to Preferences. In the Preferences window, go to the Appearance category, and then Fonts. As

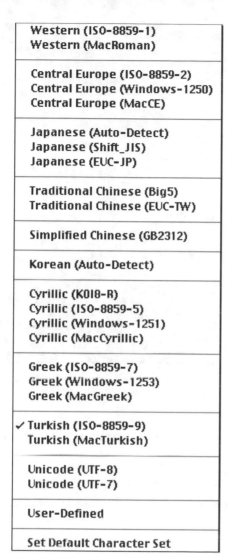

Western (ISO-8859-1) Western (MacRoman)
Central Europe (ISO-8859-2) Central Europe (Windows-1250) Central Europe (MacCE)
Japanese (Auto-Detect) Japanese (Shift_JIS) Japanese (EUC-JP)
Traditional Chinese (Big5) Traditional Chinese (EUC-TW)
Simplified Chinese (GB2312)
Korean (Auto-Detect)
Cyrillic (KOI8-R) Cyrillic (ISO-8859-5) Cyrillic (Windows-1251) Cyrillic (MacCyrillic)
Greek (ISO-8859-7) Greek (Windows-1253) Greek (MacGreek)
✓ Turkish (ISO-8859-9) Turkish (MacTurkish)
Unicode (UTF-8) Unicode (UTF-7)
User-Defined
Set Default Character Set

Figure 9.5 Character sets available in Netscape Communicator.

shown in Figure 9.6, this gives you the ability to specify variable and fixed-width fonts for each available encoding. After doing this, when you specify that you want to compose a mail message in a particular encoding (or when you receive one), the application will default to the font that you selected.

Unfortunately, only one non-Latin character set can be used in a single message. Many character sets allow for the use of Latin with the main writing system of that character set (Latin and Cyrillic, Latin and Greek, and so forth), but you could not, for example, use Cyrillic text

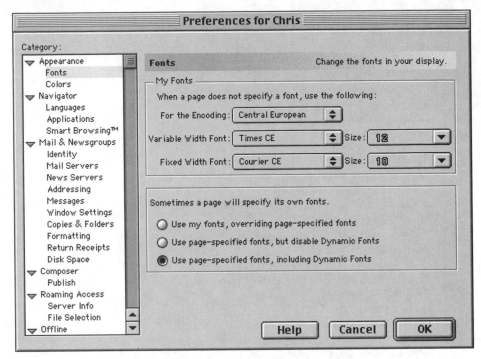

Figure 9.6 Specifying fonts for particular encodings in Netscape Communicator.

and Japanese in the same message, unless you are using the universal character set Unicode.

For additional details about sending and receiving multilingual email with Netscape Communicator, see www.fas.harvard.edu/~mittenth/ nrl_email.html.

Netscape Communicator is available for Windows, the Mac OS, and other platforms and is available in a variety of localized versions.

NOTE

Procedures described here can vary slightly from version to version and platform to platform. In particular, the Options window in Windows versions of these applications is generally the equivalent of the Preferences window in the Macintosh version (if available), and vice versa.

Email 97

Email 97, from E Corp. (www.e-corp.com), is an application for Windows 95 and higher or Windows NT. Email 97's main feature that makes it useful to multilingual users is eTranslator, which has six built-in automatic translation dictionaries for Italian, German, French, Spanish, Portuguese, and English. This feature is a part of the Email 97 Premier Edition.

Eudora

If you're willing to do a bit of customization with plug-ins and other options, Eudora, from Qualcomm (www.qualcomm.com)—one of the most widely used email applications—can handle dozens of languages.

Complete details on international add-ons, utilities, and versions of Eudora for Windows are available online at http://emailman.com/ eudora/win/util.html#international. For the Macintosh, see www.emailman.com/eudora/mac/international.html.

Outlook Express

Microsoft Outlook Express, included with Internet Explorer (www.microsoft.com), is able to identify many commonly used character sets and to display messages accordingly (if you already have support for that language installed on your computer). Figure 9.7 shows a message with Cyrillic text (written in the application Tango Mail, which is discussed next) that was identified automatically so that the message would be correctly displayed.

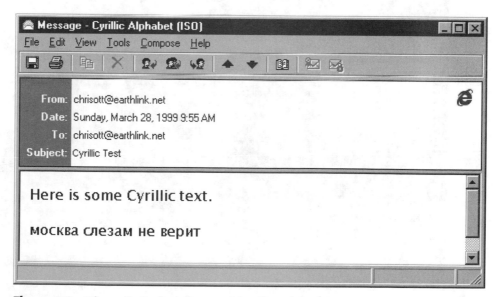

Figure 9.7 Microsoft Outlook Express identifies character sets and displays texts in an appropriate font.

If you receive a message that does not have a character set specified, you can try selecting one manually in Outlook Express. To do this, double click the message in the message list that you want to change. Then, pull down the Format menu, choose Language (Character Set in Mac OS), and choose a character set. The character set that you choose is used by Outlook Express to display the message but does not change the character set used in the message.

As shown in Figure 9.8, you follow the same procedure if you want to change the language and character set for a message that you are composing.

To specify fonts to use with a particular character set, go to the Options or Preferences window (depending on which platform you are using). As shown in Figure 9.9, you can specify which fonts you want to use with a particular character set.

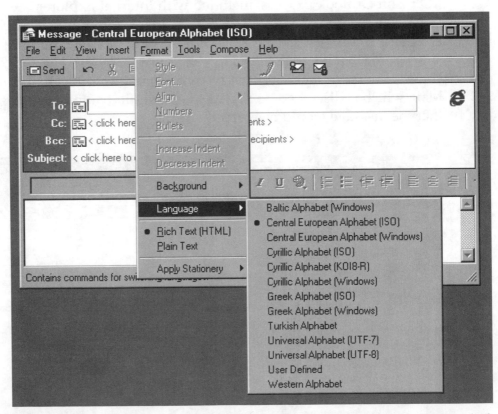

Figure 9.8 Changing the character set for a message you are writing in Microsoft Outlook Express.

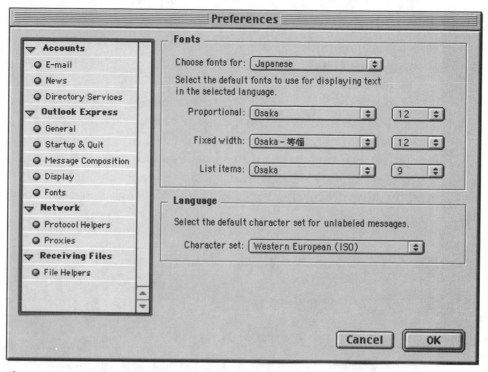

Figure 9.9 Specifying fonts for a particular character set in Outlook Express.

Version 4 of Outlook Express is somewhat more advanced than version 4 of Netscape Communicator in its ability to handle more than one writing system in the same message. In this situation, Outlook Express will prompt you about converting your message to the universal Unicode character set instead of using individual character sets.

Outlook Express is available for both Windows and the Mac OS, and is available in several localized versions.

Newsgroups

The two email offerings from Netscape and Microsoft that are described here (Communicator and Outlook Express) are a part of the version 4.0 browsers from these companies. Also included in these packages, however, is the ability to read newsgroups. Details on how to read non-Latin text in newsgroups are essentially the same as for reading non-Latin text in email messages.

Tango Mail

Tango Mail, a feature of the Tango multilingual browser from Alis Technologies (www.alis.com), is by far the most world-savvy email application that is currently available. Tango Mail includes its own input methods for different writing systems with 50 on-screen pop-up keyboards available (some shown in Figure 9.10), including phonetic and shape-based input methods for Chinese, Japanese, and Korean. All of this makes it possible to send and receive email in more than 90 languages. Email messages can also be truly multilingual by supporting the use of multiple writing systems. Other appli-

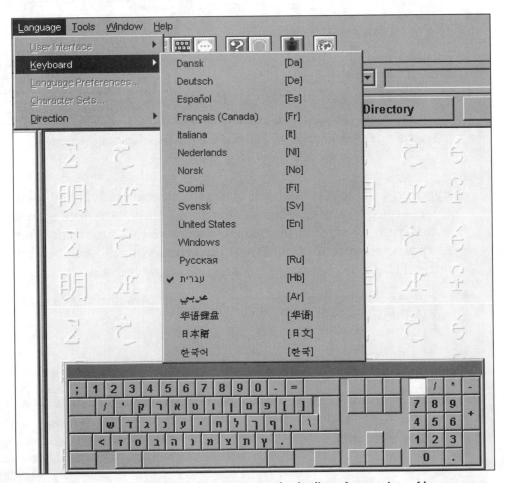

Figure 9.10 Tango Mail offers built-in input method editors for a variety of languages.

cations are limited to two (a Latin script and another script such as Cyrillic or Hebrew).

You can customize the keyboard list in Tango Mail's Keyboards submenu. To do this, pull down the Edit menu and choose Preferences. Within the Preferences window, as shown in Figure 9.11, choose Keyboards, and select the keyboards that you want to include in the keyboard lists.

Tango Mail's capabilities are available without modifying your PC or its operating system. Recipients of messages sent from Tango Mail do not need Tango Mail to read them if they have an email application that supports common mail standards and character sets, along with appropriate language support. When you send out a message created in a script that can use more than one character set, Tango will prompt you and offer the choices for the script you used before transmitting your message. Finally, Tango Mail's entire user interface and help system can be switched on the fly between 19 different languages.

Tango Mail's most significant drawback is that it is available only for Windows 3.1 and higher, not for the Mac OS, Unix, or any other platform.

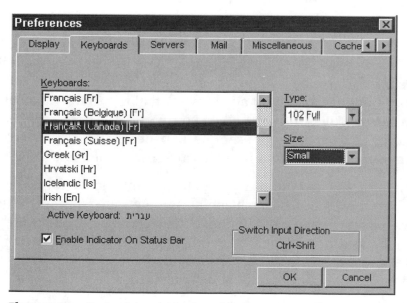

Figure 9.11 Customizing the keyboard list for Tango Mail.

Multilingual Email through Online Subscription Services

The remaining online subscription services tend to be somewhat limited in their ability to handle email written in non-Latin alphabets. CompuServe (www.compuserve.com) is generally regarded as the most capable at handling multilingual texts. MSN (http://home.microsoft.com) and AOL (www.aol.com) can handle one-byte non-Latin text as well, but they work best internally (for example, from one AOL account to another) and with as few other differences as possible. "One big factor is having compatible OS environments and systems at both ends of a link," says Stephen H. Franke, principal and integrator of the Middle East Services Group. When this doesn't work, Franke suggests converting messages with non-Latin content to plain text files and then making them readable on the other end by opening them and choosing a font that can display the characters correctly.

Interactive Forms

Support for non-Latin scripts in interactive forms on Web pages is still limited. The biggest limit is that most sites are not yet capable of handling non-Latin scripts.

For forms that are multilingual, you may be able to use non-Latin script support that is installed on your computer, or you can use the Tango browser (described in Chapter 3, "Multilingual Compatibility Issues"), which supports input for dozens of languages. Tango has the best multilingual abilities of any browser that is currently available, and it can be truly surprising when you start to see non-Latin text appearing as it should—for example, in pages that are generated dynamically based on your input, as in a search engine.

To test the ability of your browser to handle interactive forms on Web pages, try the AltaVista search engine at www.altavista.com, which allows for searches in more than two dozen languages, including Chinese, Japanese, Korean, and other languages that use non-Latin scripts. Another site with Chinese-specific search capabilities is available from SINANET, Inc., at www.sinanet.com.

Standards are still being established for the use of *combined* Unicode characters in searches, such as characters combined with diacritics, like *á*. For more details, see the draft Unicode technical reports UTR #10, "Unicode Collation Algorithm," and UTR #15, "Unicode Normalization Forms," available online at www.unicode.org/unicode/reports/techreports.html.

Multilingual Communication with PDAs and Other Wireless Devices

Although still generally limited, options for multilingual computing with handheld personal digital assistants (PDAs) and cellular phones with features such as phonebook memory are starting to become available. This section profiles some of the current offerings.

Palm Computing

One of the best-known PDAs, the Palm Computing series from 3Com, is available in a variety of international versions, including the major European languages, as well as East Asian languages such as Japanese and Korean. For more information, see the Palm Computing international page at www.palm.com/intl/index.html. The Japanese version, for example, includes English-to-Japanese and Japanese-to-English dictionaries, as well as synchronization software that supports transfers of Japanese information between a Palm device and a desktop computer.

T9 Text Input

T9 Text Input, from Tegic Communications (www.tegic.com), is software for wireless phones, pagers, and handheld organizers. It simplifies input in 13 languages, including Simplified and Traditional Chinese, and Korean. T9 is available to end users, but several manufacturers, such as Motorola and Palm Computing, have licensed T9 technology and now include it with some of their products.

Zi 8

Ericsson Mobile Communications (www.ericsson.com) has announced that all new ranges of its mobile phones will include a version that supports Chinese input technology for messaging and the electronic storage of names and numbers. Three input options that make use of the phone's keypad, developed by Zi Corporation (www.zicorp.com), are available: the phonetic Pinyin and Bopomofo methods, and a stroke-based method, in which you start by pressing keys for individual strokes until the character is complete.

Next

Having looked at purely electronic communication, such as email, the next chapter takes a look at multilingual print publishing and multilingual multimedia.

CHAPTER 10

Multilingual Publishing, Graphic Design, and Multimedia

A t first it might seem that being able to do successful multilingual publishing and graphics work requires only the ability to handle different languages with your applications. This is necessary, but success is not just a matter of being able to *do* these languages. If your work will be distributed in a variety of countries, you may also need to change procedures if the same documents and files have to be localized.

This chapter discusses the multilingual aspects of publishing, graphic design, and multimedia, with a look at the major issues involved and the applications and tools that can help you put your multilingual work in print or on screen.

Choosing Applications

One of the most basic and obvious considerations when choosing applications for multilingual publishing and graphics work is *language support*. Does an application support the languages you need to work in? It is also important to ask whether the same applications will support any languages that you may need to use in the future. You may need only the Western European languages and Japanese today, but what if you need Chinese and Hebrew a few years from now?

If the applications you use for publishing and graphics work don't support the languages that you need to work with now (or the ones that you may need to work with in the future), you will need to do one of two things: Use different applications for different language versions of the same project (which can make things considerably more complicated), or convert the existing language versions of your documents to the format for an application that is more fully multilingual.

Conversions such as this are becoming easier, thanks to built-in converters within applications (for example, Adobe's new *InDesign* software can import files from QuarkXPress) and third-party conversion software, such as *MacLinkPlus* and *Conversions Plus* (Windows) from DataViz (www.dataviz.com), but it will make the already complex process of localizing your files even more complicated. This is a consideration for any type of work, but converting from one word-processing format to another, for example, is usually easier than converting graphics and publishing files, which tend to be more complex.

It is also important to pay attention to *versions,* because it is possible that localized versions of publishing or graphics software will not be available at the same time as the latest English (or other primary-language) version. If you design a publication in the latest version of a publishing application, it may not be possible to open it with older versions, which may still be the only options available for the languages the publication needs to be localized for. Pay close attention to when the different localized versions of the publishing and graphics applications you use become available. You may want to hold off on upgrading until all the different language versions of a product you need are ready—and until printers and anyone else you need to work with have them, as well.

For all of these reasons, it is a good idea to pay close attention to the language support offered by the applications you use to make sure that your investment in these applications will not be lost if you have to convert to another format in the future. Later sections of this chapter provide details about the language support for commonly used applications.

Allowing for Expansion

When localizing a publication or project, be aware that texts translated from English to other languages can be as much as about 40 percent longer than the original version, and to some degree the same thing can happen when translating from other languages, as well. Some expansion takes place because concepts expressed in the source language may be more difficult to express concisely in another language, and not always because some languages are inherently longer. For example, a single word in the source language may require a phrase in the target language, regardless of the languages involved.

This is an important consideration to bear in mind when any text is localized (such as the text in the user interface for an application), but it can be especially important in publications that have a lot of text. The more text there is, the more expansion there can be.

The way to accommodate this is to leave extra space in the primary-language versions of publications that need to be localized. This can be done with wider margins and more space between paragraphs and columns. Depending on your document, it may be best to try to accommodate the expansion of a translated text without adding additional pages. Adding pages makes it impossible to keep uniform page references across language versions (for example, a sentence like "See page 147 for more details" will have to be changed if page numbers differ from one localized publication to another).

Publishing Considerations

Multilingual publishing is not simply a matter of translation. Going from design to paper can be a complex process for any language, but there are special considerations when publishing documents in non-Latin writing systems or for an international readership.

Allowing for Paper Size

If you are designing publications that are meant to be printed out on "standard" paper, remember that there are different standard sizes.

The A4 paper size that is commonly used outside of the United States is slightly narrower (210 mm, or 8.26 inches) and slightly taller (297 mm, or 11.693 inches) than "standard" 8.5- by 11-inch paper.

Since these sizes are close, however, you may be able to compromise by designing for the narrower dimensions from each of the two standards, such as an 8.25- by 11-inch (210- by 280-mm) document. This technique will give you wider vertical or horizontal margins, depending on which size paper you're printing on, but it will save you the trouble of having to design two slightly different page layouts.

Avoiding Hyphenation

Hyphenation isn't even possible in some languages, such as Chinese, but it is a good idea to avoid using hyphenation in documents that will be translated, even when hyphenation is possible. Automatic translation systems and translation-memory tools may stumble over hyphenated words, mistaking them for two separate elements.

Standards

Depending on the size and formality of your operation, you may have a standard corporate font. If so, do you have versions of this corporate font for non-Latin scripts? It is especially important for fonts to match—to be the same size, require the same leading (vertical space between lines), and simply look right—across languages and writing systems. This is especially true if you will be mixing text from different scripts in the same document. For example, you might include English references in a Japanese manual.

Graphics Considerations

Similarly, there are considerations that apply to graphics in multilingual work. At first it might seem that graphics would be free of multilingual problems—after all, graphics may not contain *any* language—but even "pure" graphics that are free of text may need to be reevaluated for their international appropriateness, or to make sure that they accurately depict all the localized versions of a product.

Making Graphics Generic and Culturally Sensitive

Cultural issues, such as the need to avoid icons that might not be understood in some locales (U.S. mailboxes, for example), are discussed throughout this book, and this same awareness is important for graphics, as well.

There is no comprehensive guide to all of the issues that could potentially pose a problem (their range is essentially infinite), but as a general rule, avoid depicting anything that might seem out of place in another locale where your graphics might be seen, or that might need to be changed for individual localized versions. Examples include recognizable currency or currency symbols (unless they are used with a truly global mix of other currencies), readable text (as in a photo of a stack of newspapers or anything else with text on it), and images of things that vary in appearance from country to country, such as phone booths, taxis, street signs, or public buses.

It's also important to keep graphics culturally sensitive. Maps are a potential problem, for example, if they show disputed boundaries.

For more suggestions on where to look for information about issues to avoid, see the *Microsoft's Geopolitical Product Strategy Group* sidebar in Chapter 5, "Strategies for Multilingual Development and Internationalization."

Keeping Graphics Free of Text

Because it is usually more difficult to localize text in a graphics file—you can't simply open the file and retype the text in a graphic, because it has been bitmapped (converted to pixels, as if it were just another part of the graphic) and is no longer editable as text—it is important to keep graphics as free of text as possible.

For example, when explaining the features in an application's window, your first inclination might be to insert labels in a screen shot to identify its features. For graphics that must be localized, it may make more sense to insert numbers in the screen shot near features that need to be explained. These numbers will probably not need to be localized, and you can simply refer to them in the body of your text. Isolating text from graphics in this way makes graphics easier to localize, and also avoids the problem of translated labels taking up more space and crowding the graphic.

Another reason to keep text out of graphics is that if your graphics will appear on a Web site, someone may run your site through an automatic translator. Automatic translators are unable to recognize and translate text that is embedded in a graphic. This is particularly important if your graphics are used for navigating your site.

Working in Layers

Most graphics and publishing programs now make it possible to work in layers, which can have specific attributes, and to keep content in one layer separate from content in other layers. This can be useful for producing bilingual or multilingual documents with a different layer for each language. If one or more of these languages later needs to be translated to other languages, layers can provide a convenient way to keep the different languages separate.

Providing Source Files

For occasions when it is necessary to include text (or another element that needs to be localized, such as the image of a dollar bill, a pound note, or a deutschemark) in a graphic, try to provide both the final version of your graphic and a version that has everything but the element that needs to be localized. If you can stop and save before adding any elements that need to be localized, you will save localizers the trouble of having to remove these elements before they can put in more appropriate ones.

Similarly, if you need screen shots, make sure that the graphics staff has the applications and any necessary source files (such as a database) in addition to the final source-language version of the graphic. Providing these source files will make it easier to recreate the screen shots for a localized version. If necessary, the data itself (a section of English text, dollar figures in a spreadsheet, and so forth) in the source files can be localized and opened in the localized version of the application; then a new screen shot can be made and compared against the screen shot for the primary-language version.

If the graphics professionals responsible for making these screen shots do not understand the languages of the localized applications, they will need specific instructions about how to set up the application for the screen shot.

Double Checking

Depending on who is doing your graphics work and whether they know all of the languages that they are working in, it can be extremely important to check their work for errors. Obviously, writers or translators would never work with a language with which they were completely unfamiliar, but graphics work is one of the few instances in which people who may not know a language do work involving that language.

One classic example of the kind of gaffe that can occur is when a Russian "backwards *R*" is used incorrectly, as shown in Figure 10.1. Sometimes this is merely an attempt to be cute, but it can also scream ignorance of the language. This "backwards *R*" has nothing to do with the letter *R* at all. In the Cyrillic alphabet, this character is actually a vowel, pronounced "ya."

Graphics work by designers who aren't familiar with a language needs to be checked for errors and inappropriate usage.

Another reason to be careful about checking work in multilingual publications is that graphics and translated text may have been taken out and worked on in several different applications and formats before making their way back into the document. It's important to make sure that nothing has been lost along the way.

Premium

Яussian

Vodka   **Figure 10.1** When designers get creative with languages they don't know, it can lead to inappropriate usage.

Printing

Printing with two-byte fonts can be particularly complicated. Because there can be thousands of characters, downloading them from your computer to a printer can be prohibitively slow.

To get around this, some applications rasterize (convert to pixels) the TrueType fonts used in your document and send these characters to the printer as bitmaps. You can achieve better results, however, if a PostScript (Type 1) font of the same name is installed on the printer, because this font can then be used instead of the rasterized version. If the fonts used in your document are not installed on the printer, the images that are printed may print with jagged edges. Using *Adobe Type Manager* (ATM) can correct this problem.

If you are using a service bureau (what might commonly be called a "printer" is often referred to professionally as a *service bureau* because of the range of services offered, and to distinguish it from a laser printer) to output East Asian documents, be aware that either the service bureau must have the same version of the application you are using and the fonts used in your document, or you can give the service bureau a PostScript file. This will allow it to print the file even without the same language support that you have.

Working with Service Bureaus

Multilingual work that is sent out to be printed becomes especially complicated because you not only need to set up your own systems for other languages, you have to make sure that your service bureau can handle these languages, as well.

Contact the service bureau beforehand to make sure that it has, or at least can handle, the fonts that you need. If possible, use standard, easily available fonts, or be prepared to furnish a copy of the fonts you have used if they are unique to your organization.

You may also want to consider using a service bureau that specializes in multilingual work, such as *MultiMedia PrePress* (www.mmpt.com), which specifies the languages and language versions of applications that it works with.

Working in Language Kits or a Localized OS?

Apple's family of language kits (www.apple.com/macos/multilingual/ languagekits.html) provides a convenient way for Mac OS publishers and designers to work with languages that they don't understand. Using a fully localized version of an operating system generally means that all menus, dialog boxes, and other functions have been translated to the target language. This can be very confusing if you're a graphic designer who needs to work with files that contain non-Latin text which you may not understand. Language Kits make it possible to support work in these writing systems while continuing to work in an English operating system.

Similar options exist for Windows. See Chapter 1, "The World-Ready Computer," for more details.

Publishing and Graphics Tools

This section describes the multilingual offerings of the companies that make some of the most widely used graphics and publishing applications.

Adobe

Although its flagship publishing product *PageMaker* traditionally took a back seat to QuarkXPress, in recent years Adobe has put together a family of applications that cover the entire range of print and electronic publishing. Many of these applications share similar support for multilingual text and spelling dictionaries, and are also available in localized versions for a greater number of languages than publishing and graphics products from other companies.

Information is provided about individual applications here, but for additional details and more updated information, search Adobe's site at www.adobe.com with the name of the language and application you are interested in. The company maintains an extensive online library of CustomerFirst Support pages with information about multilingual issues and many other topics. By searching for a language and application, you'll find some support pages with detailed information.

Adobe applications can also save files in Adobe's *Portable Document Format* (PDF). Fonts are embedded in PDF files, which makes it possible to view them on other computers even without appropriate language support. With any localized language version of *Acrobat 4.0* or the free *Acrobat Reader*, it is possible to view documents containing text in languages including English, French, German, Japanese, Chinese, Korean, Swedish, Spanish, Dutch, Italian, Arabic, Hebrew, and Brazilian Portuguese. This makes PDF a particularly useful format for exchanging multilingual documents.

FrameMaker

FrameMaker, Adobe's application for publishing books and other large, complex documents, has some of Adobe's most complete multilingual support.

With the appropriate language support (a localized operating system or language kit), FrameMaker offers support for double-byte characters for Japanese, Chinese, and Korean on Mac OS, Windows, and Unix. Support for Japanese text is included in all language versions of FrameMaker, and a completely localized Japanese version is available on all platforms. With appropriate language support, FrameMaker also supports Korean and Simplified and Traditional Chinese in the English-language version.

Other FrameMaker features include support for line breaking and hyphenation in Asian languages, the ability to combine Western and Asian fonts in the same paragraph, and Kanji, Hiragana, and Katakana options for page numbering, autonumbering, and footnotes in the Japanese version. For additional details, see www.adobe.com/ prodindex/framemaker/feature3.html.

Illustrator

Illustrator is Adobe's illustration software for designers, graphic artists, and technical illustrators. Its multilingual features include the ability to handle vertical text and vertical text on a path, and support for viewing, editing, and printing documents that contain Japanese text without having to switch to a Japanese operating system or a Japanese version of the application.

Illustrator is available in localized versions for languages including the major European languages, as well as Chinese, Japanese, and Korean. Most of these languages are available for both Windows and Macintosh (and some for Unix, as well), although the latest versions are not always simultaneously available for all languages. For details on availability, see www.adobe.com/prodindex/illustrator/price.html.

InDesign

Adobe's new flagship publishing product, InDesign, not yet officially released at the time of writing, is to offer the ability to work with files produced in other language versions of InDesign (International English can open French, Japanese can open French, and so forth), and with a Japanese operating system or a Japanese language kit installed, you can enter, save, and edit Japanese text in any other language version of InDesign.

InDesign also makes it possible to associate a language with a character, word, or longer text, which means that the appropriate hyphenation and spelling dictionaries will be used whenever text for a particular language is encountered in a document. It is also possible to specify language as an attribute for a character or paragraph style, which makes it possible, for example, to have quotation marks automatically converted to guillemets (« ») in a French text. In addition, documentwide layers can be used to create different language versions of the same document.

InDesign is planned to debut in localized versions including French, German, International English, Canadian English, Japanese, Swedish, Italian, Dutch, Spanish, Brazilian Portuguese, Norwegian, Finnish, and Danish. For the latest details about InDesign, see www.adobe.com/prodindex/indesign/price.html.

Photoshop

The type tool in Adobe's image-editing application, Photoshop—including the freely distributed *Photoshop LE* (Limited Edition)—handles two-byte and other non-Latin fonts without difficulty, as shown in Figure 10.2.

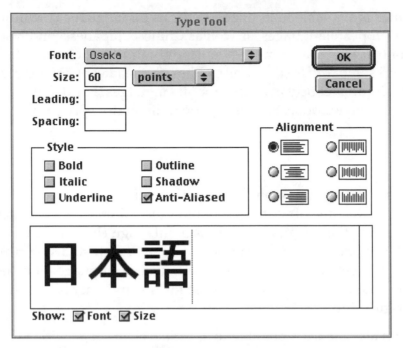

Figure 10.2 Entering Japanese text in the Photoshop Type Tool.

For other details and information about the latest localized versions of Photoshop that are currently available, see www.adobe.com/ prodindex/photoshop/prodinfo.html.

PageMaker

Adobe's page-layout software, PageMaker, is available in localized versions for almost two dozen Latin and non-Latin languages. Page-Maker supports a range of languages, including some with non-Latin alphabets, but its ability to handle two-byte languages is limited in versions that have not been localized for these languages.

With appropriate language support, you may be able to basically input text, but your ability to work with it with PageMaker's typographic tools is limited. For the latest details on PageMaker, see www.adobe .com/prodindex/pagemaker/prodinfo.html.

Quark

Quark's main offering with multilingual capabilities is its flagship product *QuarkXPress* and the related multilingual version *QuarkXPress*

Passport, which contains hyphenation and justification rules as well as dictionaries for U.S. English, International English, Danish, Dutch, French, German, Italian, Norwegian, Spanish, Swedish, and Swiss-German.

For Western European languages, single-language localized versions of QuarkXPress are available for the languages listed here, and are available for the Mac OS in Japanese, Korean, Traditional Chinese, and Simplified Chinese. These require either the matching localized version of the Mac OS itself or the corresponding language kit from Apple. For Windows, the only Asian language available is Japanese, which requires the Japanese version of the Windows operating system.

QuarkXPress and QuarkXPress Passport are limited in their ability to deal with non-Latin-alphabet languages for which localized versions are not available.

Quark is also developing *Babel,* a free XTension for users of Quark-XPress Passport who produce documents that are essentially identical in multiple languages. Babel makes it possible to export the entire document into multiple XPress documents for translators to work with. Translated text can then be reimported with all links intact, and instead of creating many single-language documents, Babel makes it possible to use multiple *language overlays*. Babel's Image Path feature also makes it possible to associate language-specific graphics with a particular language's overlay, and the SmartFit tool helps accommodate the change in the length of a document that may occur when texts are translated to other languages. For more information about the Babel XTension, see www.quark.com/quarkxpress/babelxt.html.

Diwan Software

Less well known than offerings from Adobe and Quark is Diwan Software's *Ready, Set, Go! Global* (www.diwan.com), which is nonetheless a strong multilingual publishing contender.

RSG-Global, available for the Macintosh, bundles all of Apple's language kits and allows work in all of the languages that these kits support, for truly multilingual documents. RSG-Global also has advanced multilingual typographic control and handles proper kerning and justification for each language, as well as right-to-left and vertical text.

Macromedia

FreeHand, from Macromedia (www.macromedia.com), is illustration software that is a rival to Adobe Illustrator.

To handle double-byte text in FreeHand for languages such as Chinese and Japanese, it is necessary to have a language kit or localized operating system for that language. FreeHand is available in localized versions for German, French, Spanish, Swedish, Italian, Japanese, Korean, Traditional Chinese, Hebrew, and Portuguese. The latest versions are not always available simultaneously for all localized versions.

Microsoft

The graphics and publication tools from Microsoft—*Microsoft Publisher* and *Microsoft PhotoDraw*—share the multilingual capabilities of the Microsoft Office suite, of which they are a part and which are detailed in Chapter 2, "World-Savvy Applications."

A Translation Tool for Desktop Publishing

International Translation and Publishing (www.itp.ie) and TRADOS Ireland Ltd. (www.trados.com) recently introduced the *ITP Filter Pack,* a suite of markup utilities that enable the translation of text in PageMaker, QuarkXPress, and other publishing formats with TRADOS Translator's Workbench (see Chapter 8, "Translation and Localization").

Multimedia

Developing multimedia projects is inherently complex because of the multiple dimensions involved—text, sound, video, and so forth. Things become even more complex when you add yet another dimension—*language.*

When planning a multimedia project for other languages and locales, keep the following issues in mind.

Print Considerations

Some of the same multilingual considerations that apply to print should be kept in mind for multimedia projects, as well. Be sure to allow for the expansion of text if you will be translating and localizing your project. Make sure that icons and other graphical elements are easily understandable regardless of language, as well as culturally appropriate.

Also, if possible, keep text that may need to be translated out of graphics that need to be localized. One way to improve the appearance of text, and thereby avoid the need to include it in graphics, is to use built-in text antialiasing (automatic smoothing of the on-screen appearance of text), if this feature is available in the multimedia authoring software that you use.

Multimedia Localization Is More Complex

Creating a multimedia project for a single language isn't significantly more complex for one language than it is for another. But if you need to localize a project for one or more languages, things become very complex, because all the media elements in your project may need to be translated or adapted for the target language and locale. Depending on the nature of your project, you may also have to make changes to images, video, sound recordings, and other media to make sure that they are appropriate for the audience you are trying to reach. You may also need to take into account regional differences even within a single locale, such as different accents in different parts of the same country. Depending on your project, you (or any localization service you may be working with) may need to do thorough research about the locale and make careful choices about any actors who are involved in the project. These requirements also naturally increase the cost and amount of time required to complete a project.

Another factor that can complicate localization efforts is the more free-form nature of multimedia projects. The development of traditional applications has now become relatively disciplined, and various techniques (such as storing menu names and other interface features that need to be translated in resource files that are separate from code) are relatively well known. The development of multimedia projects, on the other hand, has tended not to follow well-established procedures and can complicate localization. For this reason, you may need to allow extra time to complete a project.

Dubbing Isn't Enough

As in film, if you already have video segments in a multimedia project, you may not get good results by dubbing in voice-overs. Your efforts may resemble the much-lampooned Japanese monster movies that have been dubbed into English and in which it is obvious that what was said in the original Japanese script took longer to say than the English translation. For ideal results, you may need to reshoot your video segments with native speakers.

Depending on your project, you may want to consider the use of animation in place of live actors. It is easier to synchronize voice-overs in animation, and it is easier to extend the length of time that a character's mouth is moving with animated segments.

Another way to avoid this issue with video segments that are narrated is to make sure that the narrator is not visible. Then you can simply replace the sound track for the narrator and adjust timing for the animation or video as necessary.

Allowing Time to Investigate Legal Issues

If you are working on a project that requires sources that you don't own the rights to—for example, images, video clips, or sound recordings with historical or cultural importance—it is especially important to begin your efforts to obtain the rights to use these materials early. You'll need to allow more time to contact copyright owners in other countries.

You may also need to decide what to do in case you can't find the original owners of the rights that you seek. A particularly notorious version of this problem arises when dealing with copyrights on books, films, recordings, and so forth, produced in the Soviet Union and other now-collapsed communist governments. Since films, for example, were usually made and financed by state-owned studios, the entities that owned the rights to these works may no longer exist. In some cases, rights may have been transferred to new governments or to individuals and private companies, but it is difficult to know for sure without a great deal of research. If a project depends on archival material of some sort, it is important to sort through these legal issues with copyright experts as early as possible.

It's also important to be clear on other issues, such as laws on fair use (material for educational purposes, for example), which vary from country to country.

Making Media Elements Culturally Appropriate and Relevant

By their nature, multimedia projects can be greatly enhanced with images, sound, and video. It is important, however, to make sure that these media elements are, at least, culturally neutral or, at best, customized for each localized version of the project. Otherwise, the creativity that multimedia makes possible can, in some cases, work against successful localization.

One example of a creative product that unfortunately seemed to be designed without much thought to cultural relevance was a French language-learning CD-ROM called *Learn to Speak,* from the Learning Company. One of the games in the product takes place in a western-style saloon for a vocabulary review with a canine character named Clint Dogwood. As shown in Figure 10.3, this product was whimsi-

Figure 10.3 Try to keep multimedia scenarios culturally relevant.

cally cute—and perhaps not altogether inappropriate for the U.S. market—but the setting had nothing to do with France or the French culture. Although not intended mainly for the French market, it might have made sense to localize this product by choosing a more relevant setting for the game, such as a Parisian café.

Tools

For multilingual multimedia projects, one of the most important considerations regarding the tools you use is whether localized versions are available for the languages you need.

The large number of applications that can be used to create or contribute to multimedia work each have varying abilities to handle non-Latin writing systems. Many will handle any language that your system supports. However, whenever possible, it is best to use a fully localized version, to ensure that all aspects of your project will appear in the right language. Even if your system allows you to create a project in Japanese using the U.S. English version of a multimedia authoring tool, users of your project may encounter English dialog boxes and other text because they are embedded in the runtime engine. Be careful about letting this sort of thing slide because "Everybody knows a little English, right?"

To find a tool that fully supports the languages you need, check with the company that produces the software. Web addresses for pages with information about localized versions of some of the most commonly used multimedia authoring tools are provided in the following list:

Adobe Dynamic Media Studio (www.adobe.com/prodindex/ dynamicmedia/price.html). A suite of applications (Adobe After Effects, Illustrator, Photoshop, and Premiere) for digital video and image editing and the production of visual effects.

Apple HyperCard (www.apple.com/hypercard). A tool that makes it possible to build multimedia presentations using a series of scriptable virtual cards (essentially windows to which you can add any media element). HyperCard has full support for WorldScript and allows the use of different writing systems within the same project or text field.

Macromedia Director (www.macromedia.com/macromedia/ international/products). One of the most popular and powerful multimedia-authoring environments. Macromedia makes available a page of links useful to multilingual users of its products, including FAQs, phone numbers for offices around the world, and lists of localized products and international distributors, as well as international discussion groups for Macromedia products. See www .macromedia.com/macromedia/international.

QuarkImmedia (www.quark.com/quarkimmedia/qimfaq1 .html#dtfaq14). A multimedia and Internet-publishing add-on for the desktop-publishing application QuarkXPress. One of Immedia's main strengths is a menu-driven scripting system, which makes it easier to control media elements and interactivity. The Immedia design tool is currently available only for the Mac OS, but freely distributable players make it possible to view Immedia projects on both Mac OS and Windows systems.

SuperCard (www.incwell.com). This product, from IncWell Digital Media Group, is roughly comparable to but more sophisticated than Apple's HyperCard in its card-based approach to multimedia. IncWell plans support for Apple's language kits in SuperCard 3.6, and a fully localized Japanese version, as well.

The following tools may also be helpful for localization:

AutoPlay Menu Studio (www.indigorose.com). This tool, from Indigo Rose, is for developing AutoPlay menus for CD-ROMs and includes localization tools that allow developers to localize all text that is displayed to the user, including dialog box titles. The developer essentially creates self-contained submenus. At runtime the user's system language is identified from Control Panel settings, and the correct menu page is displayed.

L@Port (www.accentsoft.com). This Director Xtra, from Accent Software, assists with the localization of Director movies. L@Port assists with identifying the items that need translation in each of the media types that a project uses, and then reintegrating them into your project after they have been translated by a human translator.

Computer-Based Training

One multimedia product designed specifically for multilingual computer-based training (CBT) is *BlueGLAS* (Blue Shoe's Global Learning Authoring System), from Blue Shoe Technologies (www .blueshoe.com).

Available for Windows 95/98 and NT, BlueGLAS supports more than 40 languages and is designed for distance-learning projects, language education, and computer-based training modules for multilingual multinational organizations. Features include multilingual browsing and editing, and a speech-recognition engine. Projects can be distributed to students with a free runtime module.

Another well-known CBT option is *Authorware Attain,* from Macromedia (www.macromedia.com). Authorware Attain supports languages supported by the system it is used on, but for full language support in the runtime engine, you must use one of the three localized versions that are available: French, German, and Japanese.

Next

In the next, and final, chapter we turn to multilingual Internet and intranet sites.

CHAPTER 11

Creating Multilingual Internet and Intranet Sites

For the first several years of its existence, the irony of the "World Wide" Web was that it was so limited in its ability to deal with more than a handful of the world's languages. Even when it was possible to correctly display text in non-Latin scripts—or even in non–Western European alphabets—it required users to customize their browsers to be able to read this text correctly.

This situation is rapidly improving, and although multilingual Web sites can still be cumbersome to work with, both the means to create them and the browsers to view them are becoming more capable. This chapter outlines the major issues to keep in mind when developing multilingual intranet sites for global organizations, and multilingual Internet sites for the global market. It also provides information about some of the tools available.

Planning a Multilingual Web Site

A multilingual Web site can essentially multiply the advantages of having a Web site. It may be possible to multiply whatever benefits you get from having a Web site in the first place by the number of languages you translate it into. A multilingual Web site can also reduce or eliminate the cost of printing several language versions of brochures or other documents, allow you to update information more quickly (for several languages, not just one), and can help you in the online race to provide the best, most relevant content to the broadest possible linguistic audience.

There are a lot of considerations to keep in mind when planning a multilingual Web site to do all these things, but many of them are variations on the same theme: Keep in mind your potential visitors when creating it, research your international Web audience, and be prepared to respond to their suggestions about how you can make your site easier to view (by making it available using other character sets, for example).

Some of the most important issues to keep in mind when developing a multilingual site are detailed here.

Browser Minimums for the User

Although it will be up to you to create a Web site that is as convenient as possible to browse, your users will have to meet you halfway. Depending on the languages you are working with, your site's visitors will need to have at least a version 2.0 browser.

This may seem obvious, and you might be wondering who would still be using a version 2.0 browser. However, it was after version 2.0 that browsers such as Netscape Navigator began to require significantly more memory—more memory, in some cases, than some older computers had. If your site will primarily be viewed by users with fast Internet access and the latest equipment, then you don't need to worry. But depending on the region of the world or the communities you are trying to reach, only older computer models that are limited in what they can run may be available. To deal with this, you may want to provide information on your site about minimum requirements for viewing your site, as well as information about how to configure older browsers for the languages the site is presented in.

It is impossible to go into all the details for all browser versions for all languages, but what is generally involved is installing language support such as fonts for your language (which users tend to have anyway) and setting preferences to use these fonts to display certain character sets.

If most of your users will have access to version 3 or version 4 browsers or higher, so much the better. The ability of Navigator and Internet Explorer to automatically recognize pages created with other character sets and to display them correctly began to improve significantly in 1997 and 1998, especially in version 4 browsers.

Design for Quick Downloads

Depending on your audience, it may be important to design your site to download quickly, without large graphics that take a long time to transfer. This can be important even in relatively wired locations like North America, where some users may still be using older, slower modems, but it can be especially important for countries or regions where a combination of older equipment and slower Internet access can make it extremely cumbersome to download a page with several hundred kilobytes of graphics. Many Web design applications now include utilities that estimate download times at various speeds for the pages you create.

One consideration is to make sure that all graphics are accompanied by ALT tags which offer a brief description of what the graphic is, for users who turn graphics off. If possible, these ALT tags should also be translated to each of the languages that your site is localized for.

Cultural Considerations

As discussed in Chapter 5, "Strategies for Multilingual Development and Internationalization," and Chapter 10, "Multilingual Publishing, Graphic Design, and Multimedia," it is important that the contents of your Web site be as universal as possible if you are trying to reach a broad audience. It is best to avoid images or references that may be controversial, confusing, or that give the mistaken impression that your site is intended only for a specific national or local audience.

Nonnative Speakers of English

Depending on the intent of your site and the number of languages that you may localize it for, it is a good idea to keep your pages and the languages that you use on them as simple as possible. If your site has not been translated for any of the languages that some visitors to your site speak, they may have to rely on an imperfect understanding of

English or another language. If you want them to be able to use your site, it helps to keep their needs in mind.

"If you can, you need to know how your reader learned English," says Dovie Wylie, a consultant, trainer, and president of On-Site English. "They may have learned it from rock lyrics." See the *Writing Globally* section in Chapter 8, "Translation and Localization," for advice on how to make your writing easier to understand and translate for people whose command of English is limited. Well chosen icons and straight-forward design can also help users whose understanding of the languages used on your site is limited. If you want to reach these people, meet them halfway with a site that is designed for clarity and simplicity.

Dynamic Sites

Multilingual Web publishing is not just a matter of character encodings and fonts. You may also need to vary your content by language and locale, and to do this you may need to consider dynamic versus static Web pages. A *static* Web page has the same content regardless of who views it. A *dynamic* Web page is generated in response to user preferences or input (a simple example is a page of search results).

Static sites can work well for sites with perhaps only 100 or so pages, because making changes to this amount of content is a relatively manageable job. For sites larger than this, however, you may want to consider using a dynamic, database-driven site, so that when you change content for your site you only have to do it in the database for the site before making the information available through the browser. When handled this way, content changes will not generally require changes to the layout of your pages, especially if you use Web style sheets, which handle some formatting automatically. It may also be easier for nontechnical or nondesign staff to make changes to the content than if these people need to work directly with HTML. In addition, you can export your database content for use in other materials, such as brochures or catalogs.

Drawbacks to the use of dynamically generated multilingual pages are that a dynamic site is more difficult and expensive to set up (see the sections on tools later in this chapter for products that can help with this) and requires more technical skill to maintain than static Web pages, which nearly anyone can do.

It is also possible that it will be more difficult to keep central control over your content with a dynamic site. This can be an advantage—it can allow you to have more locale-specific information in pages written in languages for those locales—but it can also make the job of quality assurance more complicated when the content of your pages starts to differ from one language to the next.

Simplify a Site before Localizing

If you've run a site for a while in a single source language, consider eliminating outdated pages wherever possible to reduce the complexity of the site before localizing it. Localizing your site will mean translating it into at least one other language, or perhaps many. Anything you can eliminate before starting will save you the time, effort, and money that it would take to translate this content to other languages.

Automatic Translators

As detailed in Chapter 8, a growing number of sites offer free automatic translation services. A user can type in the URL for one of your pages and then view an automatically translated version of it.

Any text on your site that is a part of a graphic file, however, will not be translated. For example, you might have buttons for words like *search*, *next*, or *products*, as shown in Figure 11.1. To keep your site as translatable as possible, avoid the use of text in graphics in favor of easily understood icons or plain text links.

Text and Graphics

In general, it's a bad idea to include text in bitmapped graphics, because it is more difficult to translate and change, and is impossible for automatic translators to deal with. Using bitmapped graphics instead of text also increases download time, and, of course, the text in a graphic is not searchable.

Figure 11.1 Automatic translators can't translate text in graphics.

One instance in which you might be tempted to use text as a graphic, however, is if you want to ensure that anyone will be able to read your text, regardless of what language support they have for their browser. This will work, but it's not an ideal solution.

If using the standard character sets for different writing systems (described later in this chapter) doesn't work well for you (if those you need to communicate with are using nonstandard character sets, for example), you might want to consider other alternatives. One is to use a file format that allows you to embed fonts (Adobe Acrobat, QuarkImmedia, and others described later in this chapter), or to use a tool like Bitstream WebFont Maker, also described in more detail later in this chapter.

If you must use text as a graphic, try to keep it to a minimum. A good idea might be to use it only to identify your site and to provide instructions for how to view your site in a more flexible format.

Avoiding Locale-Specific Assumptions

Web sites intended for an international audience can cause confusion if they are locale-specific but you don't make it clear which locale you are talking about. For example, if you say that your tech-support department is available to respond to email between 8 A.M. and 6 P.M., what time zone do you mean? Visitors to your site may be able to guess, but it may be difficult for them to know what time zone, or even which continent, you are talking about. Be as specific as possible when giving details that are locale-dependent, and don't make assumptions.

It's also important to avoid making assumptions when designing any interactive forms that your site uses. If you ask visitors to enter their addresses, make sure that they can do it completely. For example, offer the option of including a province, prefecture, or county in place of a state. Also, make sure to ask for the user's country (addresses aren't much good without that if you can't guess from the city), for the country code for their phone number, and all other pertinent information. Tailor the name fields on interactive forms to the customs of the locales you are trying to reach: You may need to accommodate multipart last names, the placement of family names first, patronymics (in Russian and some other languages, people use forms of their father's first name in addition to the family name), or single names that serve as both a first and last name. For example, some Web forms will not allow you to advance before submitting required information. Make sure these requirements are reasonable for the locales you are trying to solicit responses from.

Organizing Your Site for Easier Localization and Language Management

How should a site that is translated into several languages be organized? A technique that works well is to put the translated pages for different language versions of a site into individual directories.

This has a number of advantages. One of the most important is that if you don't change any of the file names or their positions relative to one another within the hierarchy of your site, you won't have to change any of the links in your site even as you create different localized versions of the same pages. Figure 11.2 illustrates a simple site organized in this way.

Obviously, content within these pages can vary as necessary when it is translated, but because the structure remains the same, it becomes easier to maintain and refer to. For example, you will know that whatever information is on page *../english/a1.html* will also be available on *../french/a1.html* and *../german/a1.html*.

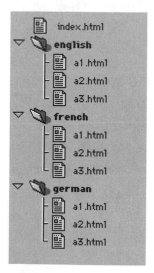

Figure 11.2   Using the same directory structure makes multilingual sites easier to maintain.

If you use this site structure, you may want to use language-neutral page names (such as a1 in this example) to avoid the need to translate. You may also want to do this for the language directory names. If you must use actual language names (english, french, spanish, and so forth) it may be best to compromise and keep them in English for the sake of simplicity, or at least to leave out diacritics. Using the correct target-language versions for these languages (français, español, and so forth) would be ideal, but this introduces characters that may cause problems because they may not be allowed by your server (as shown in Figure 11.3). In most cases, the use of non-Latin text for directory or file names will be completely impossible because current file systems deal only with ASCII text.

Depending on the purpose of your site, you may need to deviate from this approach a little or a lot. Using the same structure for different language versions of your site works well if different language versions of your site are simply meant to mirror your English content, but you may need to organize pages differently for different languages if your international content is based on a subset of your English site or if you need to develop unique content for each locale. For example, some of your products and services may not be available internationally or not in every locale, or details about meetings or job openings might be relevant only to specific locales.

Keeping Localization in Mind

Christopher Hanaoka, director of worldwide research and development for Bowne Global Solutions, cautions that developers of Web-based applications may need to be trained in (or reminded of) the development considerations that need to be kept in mind for localization, such as keeping text strings easy to localize. Web developers, many of whom are new to any kind of development, may be unfamil-

Figure 11.3 Special characters and non-Latin text are not allowed as directory or file names by many Web servers.

iar with ways to avoid problems down the line when it comes time to localize their applications. "I see a lot of the problems that we stopped seeing a few years ago starting to emerge with JavaScript, VisualBasic script and things like that," Hanaoka says. For more information about keeping localization in mind during Java development, see "Java Localization with Resource Bundles," by John O'Conner, an article that appeared in *MultiLingual Computing & Technology* (volume 9, issue 5, pages 49 to 53), as well as Chapter 5.

New Capabilities and the Web's Multilingual Future

Lately there's been a lot of talk about a possible successor to HTML called *Extensible Markup Language* (XML). Both are similar and are subsets of *Standard Generalized Markup Language* (SGML), a more comprehensive specification for the electronic storage of text, not just for the Web, but XML's advantage over HTML is its extensibility. XML makes it possible to define tags within the context of a single document instead of relying on a set of predefined tags. This makes XML more flexible and powerful than HTML.

The good news about XML for multilingual users is that XML text support is based on Unicode, not Latin text as in early versions of HTML. If XML begins to replace HTML as the main standard in use for the Web, all languages that are a part of Unicode will be supported.

At the same time, the latest specification for HTML, version 4.0, has adopted the ISO/IEC:10646 standard (essentially the same as Unicode). HTML 4.0 also has new features that are useful for multilingual purposes, such as the LANG attribute, which specifies the base language of an element in an HTML document, and which can assist in search, speech synthesis, typography, hyphenation, spell-checking, and other issues.

For example, the following simple HTML code designates a page as an English (en) page, but one paragraph is designated as French (fr), with Spanish (es) inside it.

```
<HTML lang="en">
<HEAD>
<TITLE>The HTML 4.0 LANG Attribute</TITLE>
</HEAD>
```

```
<BODY>
<P>This text is interpreted as English because English has been
designated as the default language for the document.
<P lang="fr">This text is interpreted as French because French is
specified for this particular paragraph, while <EM lang="es">this
specially tagged segment within the French paragraph</EM> is interpreted
as Spanish.
<P>With no language specified, interpretation defaults back to English.
</BODY>
</HTML>
```

See Appendix A, "Language Codes and Character Sets," for a list of two-letter language codes.

In addition, HTML 4.0 provides an easier way than Unicode to specify language direction for text and tables—the DIR attribute, used with the values LTR (left to right) and RTL (right to left). For example, in an English document that requires a Hebrew quotation, you might use the following line:

```
<Q lang="he" dir="rtl">Hebrew quotation.</Q>
```

For more details on language information and text direction in HTML 4.0, see the HTML 4.0 specification at www.w3.org.

Building Web Pages with Non-Latin Scripts

After taking into consideration the issues discussed here, creating Web pages that include non-Latin scripts is not that much different from creating pages for English, at least for HTML pages. This section discusses the main difference—the need to include CHARSET metatags— along with a few other issues.

Including CHARSET Tags on All Pages

Most Web browsers are now able to read tags built into Web pages that identify the character set needed to view and automatically display them correctly if the right fonts are available. To do this, you need to use HTML's CHARSET tag.

CHARSET is a *metatag*—a tag that describes the content of a page— and it is used within a page's HEAD tag. The HTML code for a page to display a brief text in Czech (the words *Czech Republic* in Czech) using the Central European character set ISO-8859-2 would be:

```
<html>
<head>
  <meta http-equiv="Content-Type" content="text/html;
charset=iso-8859-2">
  <title>czsample.html</title>
</head>
<body>
<font face="Palatino CE, Times New Roman CE"><font size=+3>»esk·
republika</font></font>
</body>
</html>
```

You can simply insert this CHARSET tag into the metatags for your own pages. For more information about CHARSETs for different languages, see Appendix A.

You can also specify fonts using the FONT FACE tag. Palatino CE is a common Central European font for the Mac OS, and Times New Roman CE ships with Windows. Figure 11.4 shows how this page automatically displays correctly in Internet Explorer 4 for Windows.

Figure 11.5 shows the same page in Netscape Navigator 4.5 for the Mac OS. Different platforms, applications, and fonts can be accommodated by the same page.

Finally, Figure 11.6 shows the same page without the CHARSET and FONT FACE tags—almost right, but not quite.

Specifying a font in the FONT FACE tag can be tricky because it is impossible to know whether someone visiting your site will have the

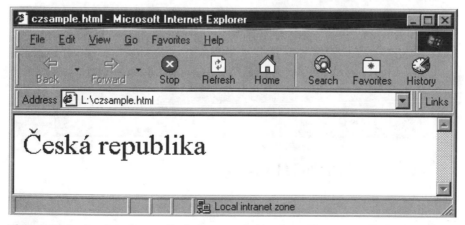

Figure 11.4 A tagged page displays correctly in Microsoft Internet Explorer for Windows.

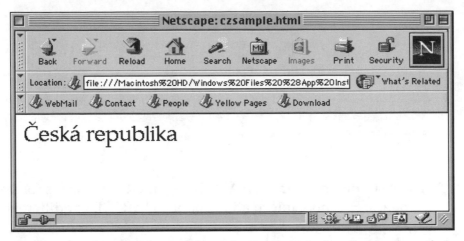

Figure 11.5 The tagged page shown in Figure 11.4 also displays correctly in Netscape Navigator for the Mac OS.

fonts that you specify (unless you are dealing with an intranet where you know that every user has a standard set of fonts installed). You can, however, specify more than one font if you know of several good possibilities, and even if you don't specify a font that the user has, it is possible that they will have set up their browser to use an appropriate font by default when it encounters the character set that you have specified for your page. You may also want to include instructions for how to do this on your site. See Chapter 2, "World-Savvy Applications," for more details.

Don't rely exclusively on the FONT FACE tag. If you create an HTML document with a particular font and specify this font in the FONT

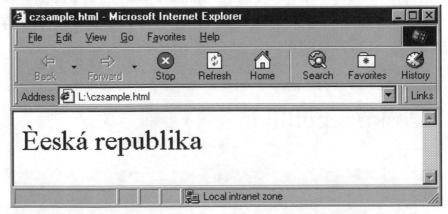

Figure 11.6 The same page shown in Figures 11.4 and 11.5 without proper language and font tagging.

FACE tag, other users who have this font will be able to read your page, but others won't, even if they have another font that would work. Specifying a CHARSET offers a way around this problem because any browser that recognizes this tag can be made to default to an appropriate font that is installed on the user's system. In other words, you can make pages without the FONT FACE tag, but not without the CHARSET tag.

The good news is that, in general, you will usually not have to deal directly with CHARSET tags and codes. A variety of Web page authoring applications described later in this chapter can insert these CHARSET tags and codes automatically.

Another promising development is that the universal character set ISO 10646-1 (essentially the same as Unicode) is the base character set for the HTML 4.0 standard. As this comes into more widespread acceptance, it is possible that the need to be concerned about character sets will fade into the background. Any visitor to your site will be able to correctly display any language you use without switching character sets, as long as they have a matching font.

It's a good idea to make sure that even your pages that use only English include a CHARSET tag, too. Currently, browsers tend to continue using the character set of the last page they have viewed. If a user switches to an English page that doesn't specify the character set ISO-8859-1 (for English and other Western European languages), the page may display the page incorrectly in the character set for another language.

NOTE

Another option for specifying fonts for your Web pages is to use a tool like Bitstream WebFont Maker, described later in this chapter.

Testing

After creating your pages, it is a good idea to test them as widely as possible, with as many different browsers (including older versions) on as many different platforms as possible. While you will not be able to test every possible system configuration that a visitor to your site may use, you can cover the most common options and either make adjustments to your site (making it available for different character sets, for example) or post instructions on how to overcome any difficulties that may arise.

HTML Authoring Tools

HTML authoring applications abound, but the following tools have strong abilities to handle multilingual content in HTML and their own advantages:

Microsoft Office 2000. A well-known and widely used tool.

Netscape Composer. A free cross-platform tool.

Tango Creator. The most complete and sophisticated tool.

Microsoft Office 2000

The Microsoft Office 2000 suite (www.microsoft.com/office), with built-in support for Unicode and other encodings, as well as bidirectional language support and the ability to save documents in HTML, has become a strong candidate for multilingual HTML authoring. Office 2000 makes handling multilingual Web content as easy as working with multilingual text in a word processor, and indeed, both can be done within the same application.

Netscape Composer

Included with Netscape Communicator (www.netscape.com) is Composer, a Web page authoring tool with broad multilingual support. Composer allows you to choose a character set (including Unicode for the support of multiple writing systems) in which to create your documents, and it automatically inserts the proper CHARSET tag so that your document can be recognized and viewed correctly by others.

NO EDIT Tags

Some Web authoring tools that are not particularly well suited to multilingual use may interfere with your text by converting non-Latin characters to raw HTML. This makes them impossible for browsers to render correctly, even when using the character set they were encoded in. A way around this is to surround your non-Latin text with <!--NOEDIT--><!--/NOEDIT--> tags. For more information, see an online tutorial about this issue at http://lang.swarthmore.edu/mellon/nonwest.

Tango Creator

Tango Creator, from Alis Technologies (www.alis.com), is one of the strongest multilingual HTML authoring solutions available. With complete support for nearly every character set, including Unicode, as well as its own built-in input methods with 50 supported keyboard layouts and the ability to customize the language of the application's user interface on the fly, the most significant drawback to Tango Creator is that it is available only for Windows 95 and higher, and not for other platforms.

Other Tools

There can be a lot more to building a multilingual Web site than HTML. These other tools can help with the development, localization, testing, and management of a site.

Microsoft BackOffice (http://microsoft.com/backoffice). This product, which includes *Site Server* for intranet publishing and management, the *Site Server Commerce Edition* for Internet commerce translations, and *SQL Server* for database and data-warehousing solutions, is available in different language versions. SQL Server also now supports Unicode, making it easier to store data in multiple languages and writing systems in the same database. For more information, see http://microsoft.com/backoffice/international/default.htm.

Global Sight Ambassador (www.global-sight.com). This product helps streamline the development and maintenance of a multilingual Web site through the use of code templates for multiple languages. Global Sight Ambassador provides an extraction utility to separate HTML code from the content of your Web pages. The content is then stored in a multilingual database for content developers and translators to work with, without having to deal with the code or cut and paste translated content into HTML pages. Database content is used to dynamically create Web pages based on the language of the user.

HtmlQA. This product is a quality-assurance tool for localizing HTML-based online help systems for Windows, from Translation Craft (www.tcraft.com/htmlqa.html). HtmlQA performs consistency checks across localized HTML projects to make sure that they function identically, and automatically checks for formatting errors.

HtmlQA supports HTML specifications through version 4.0 and common character sets. HtmlQA also searches for untranslated target text and can help with project management by locating missing and orphaned (unlinked-to) files.

QuarkImmedia. Web pages created with this product, from the maker of desktop-publishing giant QuarkXPress (www.quark.com), have the drawback of requiring a viewer (freely available for Mac and Windows), but the Mac-only QuarkImmedia authoring environment does allow for the same exacting typographic control as QuarkXPress. If they are supported by the version of QuarkXPress you use, you can embed fonts in a QuarkImmedia project so that users can view them regardless of the language support available on their own systems.

Oracle8 National Language Support (www.oracle.com/st/ o8collateral/html/xnls3twp.html). This product makes it possible to store, process, and retrieve multilingual data, and to maintain Oracle8 databases for 46 languages using 190 different character sets. It provides 63 linguistic sorting options for different locales and adapts database utilities, error messages, and date, time, and other formats to the user's language and locale.

Shopping Cart (www.webgenie.com). This product, from WebGenie, makes it possible to create a customizable online catalog and electronic shopping system with CGI support for multiple languages, including built-in support for English, French, German, Spanish, Norwegian, and Portuguese, and the ability to add custom support for an unlimited number of other languages.

SYSTRAN Enterprise (www.systranet.com). This is a client/server translation product designed for use on an intranet, extranet, or LAN. It uses the same translation engine as SYSTRAN's stand-alone software (see Chapter 8), and allows company employees to translate Web content, email, and other documents. SYSTRAN Enterprise is compatible with Windows 95 and higher or Windows NT with a Java 1.1–compliant browser, with the server running on Windows NT 4.0 or higher. Translations are available to and from English and languages including French, Italian, German, Spanish, Portuguese, Japanese, and Korean.

TagEditor. This tool, from Trados (www.trados.com), is designed to work closely with Trados Translator's Workbench (see Chapter 8), and assists with the translation of tagged documents, such as HTML and SGML files. The application allows you to drag documents from Microsoft Internet Explorer directly into TagEditor, and includes an Internet Explorer preview mode to check how your translated document will appear in a browser.

TransWeb Express. This set of utilities, from Berlitz (www.berlitz.ie/twe), is designed specifically for localizing HTML files, particularly HTML help files that may accompany a product. TransWeb analyzes localized versions of an HTML project for possible errors and inconsistencies, highlights text that needs to be translated, and reduces testing time by making it possible to view a localized version of an HTML document side by side with the source document.

WebCog Commerce. This software package, from Turnaround Computing (www.turn.com/catalog2/xlngcat3.htm), is for creating multilingual online catalogs in any language that can be presented by HTML. WebCog allows the Webmaster to enter translated text for any text string in as many languages as the site needs to support, and the HTML for each language is stored in a separate directory. WebCog also supports Unicode and the use of separate databases when different character sets must be used for different languages.

WebFont Maker. This product, from Bitstream (www.bitstream.com/products/world/webfont/index.html), allows you to add fonts to pages that will be displayed on version 4.0 browsers and higher even when the user doesn't have your fonts. The tool turns the fonts that you use to create your pages into dynamic fonts that can be displayed on the Web through a format called *portable font resource* (PFR). Using the HTML FONT FACE tag, you specify a PFR font that you have created and then direct the browser to download it from your site.

The result is that whatever fonts you use to design your page are the fonts that users will see in their browsers. Dynamic fonts download faster than using bitmapped graphics and are also preserved as searchable text.

WebPlexer. This language server, from Language Automation Inc. (www.lai.com), is designed to make it easier to create and maintain multilingual sites. WebPlexer has tools for automatic country and language navigation on a site, as well as for managing and updating multilingual content, presenting multilingual forms, and logging the country and language demographics of visitors to your site.

WorldServer. This tool, from Idiom Technologies (www.idiomtech .com), is for developing and managing global Web sites that can be integrated with an existing Web development environment. It allows Web developers to maintain a single code-base, and handles the transfer of Web content to and from translators without requiring developers to extract text from a site for translation or to integrate the translations back into the globalized site.

XML::Parser. This Perl module, available from O'Reilly & Associates (www.oreilly.com), enables the use of XML. Perl and XML::Parser are Unicode-aware, which allows XML documents written using Perl to contain non-Latin text in scripts.

For More Information

For more information about creating multilingual Web sites, see Babel (www.isoc.org:8080), a joint project of the Internet Society and Alis Technologies. The site contains advice about creating multilingual Internet sites and content, along with links to technical specifications that deal with language issues on the Web.

For a tutorial from Sun Microsystems on internationalizing Java applications—setting locales, isolating locale-specific data, formatting, working with text, and other issues—see http://java.sun.com/docs/books/tutorial/i18n/index.html.

An excellent and free white paper, "Multilingual Means Multi-Business: How to Build and Maintain a Successful Multilingual Web Presence," is available from Foreign Exchange Translations at www.fxtrans .com/faq.htm. This paper offers advice on planning, maintaining, and marketing multilingual Web sites.

Conclusion

Multilingual computing is a vast subject, and this entire book could be written again many times over just to expand on details for individual languages. For further information, all of the links to additional online information mentioned in this book are included on the companion Web site at www.wiley.com/compbooks/ott.

Language Codes and Character Sets

T able A.1 shows the two-letter language codes (from the ISO 639 standard) as well as commonly used character sets for a variety of widely used languages.

The Unicode character set supports nearly all of the world's languages and allows the display of characters from multiple writing systems when appropriate fonts are installed. When the use of Unicode is not possible, however, this table can be used to determine if the languages you need to work in can be supported by a single character set. For example, Simplified Chinese, Russian, and English are supported by the GB 2312-80 character set, so you could create Web pages or email messages using all of these languages with this character set. English and a few other languages which use the same characters as English have the widest possible compatibility with other character sets.

Many (but not all) of the character sets listed for each language are mutually compatible, such as ISO-8859-1 and Windows-1252.

Table A.1 ISO 639 Language Codes and Commonly Used Character Sets for Various Languages

LANGUAGE	LANGUAGE CODE	CHARACTER SETS
Afrikaans	af	ISO-8859-1, ISO-8859-3, Windows-1252
Albanian	sq	ISO-8859-1, ISO-8859-2, Windows-1250, Windows-1252
Arabic	ar	ISO-8859-6, Windows-1256
Azerbaijani	az	ISO-8859-5, ISO-8859-6
Basque	eu	ISO-8859-1, Windows-1252
Bulgarian	bg	ISO-8859-5
Byelorussian	be	ISO-8859-5
Catalan	ca	ISO-8859-1, ISO-8859-3, Windows-1252
Chinese (Simplified)	zh	GB 2312-80, HZ-GB-2312, ISO-2022-CN, Windows-936
Chinese (Traditional)	zh	Big5, CNS 11643-92, ISO-2022-CN, X-EUC-TW, Windows-950
Croatian	hr	ISO-8859-2, Windows-1250
Czech	cs	ISO-8859-2, Windows-1250
Danish	da	ISO-8859-1, ISO-8859-4, Windows-1252
Dutch	nl	ISO-8859-1, ISO-8859-3, Windows-1252
English	en	ASCII, Big5, GB 2312-80, GBK, ISO-8859-1, ISO-8859-3, ISO-8859-4, ISO-8859-5, ISO-8859-6, ISO-8859-7, ISO-8859-8, JIS-Roman, KOI8-R, KOI8-U, KSC-5636, TIS 620-2533, Windows-1252
Esperanto	eo	ISO-8859-3
Estonian	et	ISO-8859-4, ISO-8859-10, Windows-1257
Faeroese	fo	ISO-8859-1, Windows-1252
Finnish	fi	ISO-8859-1, ISO-8859-4, Windows-1252
French	fr	ISO-8859-1, Windows-1252
Gaelic	ga	ISO-8859-1, Windows-1252
Galician	gl	ISO-8859-1, ISO-8859-3, Windows-1252
German	de	ISO-8859-1, ISO-8859-2, ISO-8859-4, ISO-8859-3, Windows-1250, Windows-1252
Greek	el	GB 2312-80, GBK, JIS X0208, ISO-8859-7, Windows-1253
Gujarati	gu	ISCII

Table A.1 *(Continued)*

LANGUAGE	LANGUAGE CODE	CHARACTER SETS
Hawaiian	*	ASCII, Big5, GB 2312-80, GBK, ISO-8859-3, ISO-8859-4, ISO-8859-5, ISO-8859-6, ISO-8859-7, ISO-8859-8, JIS-Roman, KOI8-R, KOI8-U, KSC-5636, TIS 620-2533
Hebrew	he	ISO-8859-8, Windows-1255
Hindi	hi	ISCII
Hungarian	hu	ISO-8859-2, Windows-1250
Icelandic	is	ISO-8859-1, Windows-1252
Indonesian	id	ASCII, Big5, GB 2312-80, GBK, ISO-8859-3, ISO-8859-4, ISO-8859-5, ISO-8859-6, ISO-8859-7, ISO-8859-8, JIS-Roman, KOI8-R, KOI8-U, KSC-5636, TIS 620-2533
Inuit (Eskimo languages)	*	ISO-8859-10
Irish	ga	ISO-8859-1, Windows-1252
Italian	it	ISO-8859-1, ISO-8859-3, Windows-1252
Japanese	ja	EUC-JP, GB 2312-80, GBK, ISO-2022-JP, JIS-Roman, JIS X0201, JIS X0208, JIS X0212, Shift-JIS, Windows-932
Kazakh	kk	ISO-8859-5
Kirghiz	ky	ISO-8859-5
Korean	kr	EUC-KR, ISO-2022-KR, KSX-1001, KSC-5636, Windows-949
Kurdish	ku	ISO-8859-6
Lapp	*	ISO-8859-4, ISO-8859-10
Latin	la	ASCII, Big5, GB 2312-80, GBK, ISO-8859-3, ISO-8859-4, ISO-8859-5, ISO-8859-6, ISO-8859-7, ISO-8859-8, JIS-Roman, KOI8-R, KOI8-U, KSC-5636, TIS 620-2533
Latvian	lv	ISO-8859-4, ISO-8859-10, Windows-1257
Lithuanian	lt	ISO-8859-4, ISO-8859-10, Windows-1257
Macedonian	mk	ISO-8859-5
Malay	ms	ISO-8859-6
Maltese	mt	ISO-8859-3
Moldavian	mo	ISO-8859-5
Mongolian	mn	ISO-8859-5

* Not included in ISO 639.

Continues

Table A.1 ISO 639 Language Codes and Commonly Used Character Sets for Various Languages (Continued)

LANGUAGE	LANGUAGE CODE	CHARACTER SETS
Norwegian	no	ISO-8859-1, ISO-8859-4, Windows-1252
Pashto	ps	ISO-8859-6
Persian (Dari)	*	ISO-8859-6
Persian (Farsi)	fa	ISO-8859-6
Polish	pl	ISO-8859-2, Windows-1250
Portuguese	pt	ISO-8859-1, Windows-1252
Romanian	ro	ISO-8859-2, Windows-1250
Russian	ru	GB 2312-80, GBK, ISO-8859-5, JIS X0208, KOI8-R, KOI8-U, Windows-1251
Scottish	gd	ISO-8859-1, Windows-1252
Serbian	sr	ISO-8859-5
Sindhi	sd	ISO-8859-6
Slovak	sk	ISO-8859-2, Windows-1250
Slovenian	sl	ISO-8859-2, Windows-1250
Spanish	es	ISO-8859-1, ISO-8859-3, Windows-1252
Swahili	sw	ASCII, Big5, GB 2312-80, GBK, ISO-8859-3, ISO-8859-4, ISO-8859-5, ISO-8859-6, ISO-8859-7, ISO-8859-8, JIS-Roman, KOI8-R, KOI8-U, KSC-5636, TIS 620-2533
Swedish	sv	ISO-8859-1, ISO-8859-4, Windows-1252
Tadzhik	tg	ISO-8859-5
Thai	th	TIS 620-2533, Windows-874
Turkish	tr	ISO-8859-3, ISO-8859-9, Windows-1254
Turkmen	tk	ISO-8859-5
Ukrainian	uk	ISO-8859-5, KOI8-U
Urdu	ur	ISO-8859-6
Uzbek	uz	ISO-8859-5
Vietnamese	vi	VISCII, Windows-1258
Yiddish	yi	ISO-8859-8

* Not included in ISO 639.

The ISO-8859-1 character set is also known as *Latin 1*, and ISO-8859-2 is also known as *Latin 2*.

The ANSI character set is essentially the same as Windows-1252 and ISO-8859-1 (Latin 1).

ISO-8859-6 and ISO-8859-8 have two variants (-i, and -e), which specify whether the text's directionality is implicit in the text or explicitly encoded.

The Mac OS supports Unicode, most of the ISO encodings shown in Table A.1, and most Windows encodings, but you may encounter some older Macintosh-specific encodings as well, such as X-Mac-Roman (for Western European languages), X-Mac-CE (for Central European languages), X-Mac-Cyrillic, X-Mac-Greek, and X-Mac-Turkish.

What's on the Web Site

The companion Web site for this book at www.wiley.com/compbooks/ ott contains all the links mentioned in the book. Each chapter has its own page.

Having all of these links available online is meant to save you the trouble of typing in hundreds of URLs yourself, as well as to provide a conveniently organized gateway to additional information.

You can also watch the site for corrections and additions that couldn't be included in the print edition of the book.